Hitler Was a Socialist

A Comparison of NAZI-Socialism,

Communism, Socialism, and the United States

By Dumitru Sandru
Artwork by Dumitru Sandru
Introduction by Wolfram Klawitter

Chivileri Publishing

Copyright © 2020 by Dumitru Sandru

102820

Dumitru Sandru

https://www.sandru.com

https://www.chivileri.com

Table of Contents

Introduction

According to secular history, ever since humanity developed writing around 2700 BC, records document wars between people, tribe against tribe, cities or states against other states or nations. And with the development of agriculture and industry, people had not only the resources to support war but an incentive to make war on their neighbors to confiscate their resources. Whether these resources came in material form or human potential (slaves) or as any other means to increase production, the purpose was always the same: to increase one's wealth at the expense of somebody else, too often including the suffering of their own people. Naturally, as in almost all wars, common people fought, bled, and died, while the leadership—lords and kings and the privileged elite—benefitted almost exclusively. As populations and societies grew in number, so did the sophistication of warfare, the reasons for war, and the methods of convincing one's own citizens of the benefit thereof.

With the advent of the industrial revolution, more and more people migrated from rural areas into cities, with their factories, to make a living, placing various segments of society—the workers, the leaders, the-haves, and the-have-nots—in close proximity, thereby clearly exposing the inequities in society and eventually, during the nineteenth century, leading to the creation of labor unions and the concept of Socialism to counter Capitalism.

Socialism, according to Wikipedia, "is a political, social and economic philosophy encompassing a range of economic and social systems characterized by social ownership of the means of production and workers' self-management," which clearly advocates that the means of production and distribution should be owned by the community and not individuals, even if individuals created the company or business entity.

Well, no matter how noble the thought that all property was to be equally shared by the community, it still begs the question: Who runs, or better, who owns the community? Besides, looking at our Mother Earth, overburdened with explosive population growth, disastrous pollution, and climate change, neither Socialism nor Capitalism have so far offered any real solutions. Both concepts are materialistic in their approach to the way they treat our planet and exploit its resources. The only difference between Socialism and Capitalism is in the concept of distribution.

Nevertheless, from a political perspective, the concept of Socialism is greatly beneficial as you can make all kinds of promises to your constituents. However, once you are in power as the elected official, in almost all cases, these promises are utterly meaningless. Therefore, Socialism is not a ticket to heaven.

On the contrary, a look at the twentieth century reveals that the four political mass murderers with the highest body counts of their *own* people, their *own* citizens, were all Socialists. Starting with number one, Mao Zedong; followed by Joseph Stalin; and in a distant third Adolph Hitler, with Pol Pot trailing in the numbers of atrocities committed—atrocities committed against their own people, not people killed during times of war.

Yes, their individual brands of Socialism might have varied, but their ruthless implementation and the way their socialistic governments functioned had deadly consequences for millions of their own people.

In their socialistic forms of government there was absolutely no hint, as in the American Declaration of Independence, "that all men are created equal, that they are endowed by their Creator with certain inalienable Rights, that among these are Life, Liberty and the pursuit of Happiness." No First or Second Amendment, as in the American Constitution. As a matter of fact, if you were caught violating those rules when those Socialists were in power, you would face dire consequences and most likely death.

Unfortunately, for political reasons, only one of these murderers listed above is still vilified today: Adolf Hitler. In fact, being called Adolf Hitler or a NAZI has become a curse or an insult used by some in the political arena to describe or vilify other people of a different political opinion, even though most people do not realize who and of what political affiliation Adolf Hitler really was. Little do people know that Hitler was a devout Socialist, not a Fascist. Please keep in mind that the word NAZI stands for *National Socialism*, not National Fascism. Therefore, this book will demonstrate that Adolf Hitler was a socialist— one of the most dangerous kind. In addition, the book will highlight some of the differences of the various other forms of dangerous Socialism: Marxism, Communism, and Bolshevism.

Introduction by Wolfram Klawitter

Extraordinary Note:

This book, "Hitler Was A Socialist", created a lot of consternation among the Marxists-Socialists and some of the Amazon employees in the advertising and reviewing departments.

At first, the Amazon Media Services in charge of advertising on Amzon.com has prevented my book from being advertised. It took an act of *Jeff Bezos*, to make them see that advertising is commerce, not political ideology and censorship.

All 1-Star reviews for this book are ideological reviews from Marxist-Socialists who did not buy or read this book, and to this author's amazement they do not know what socialism is, or its horrific history. Furthermore, the nameless reviewing committee members have blocked the higher star reviews from being posted, allowing mostly the 1-Star reviews, without proof of purchase.

Read this book and find out what the Marxists-Socialists are afraid of.

Chapter 1. Hitler Was a Socialist?

WTF? Adolf Hitler was a Socialist? Preposterous! Blasphemy against the International Socialist Cause! Who would say a thing like that?

As noted in "Adolf Hitler" by John Toland, Adolf Hitler in 1927, at Clou restaurant center in Berlin said:

We are socialists, we are enemies of today's capitalistic economic system for the exploitation of the economically weak, with its unfair salaries, with its unseemly evaluation of a human being according to wealth and property instead of responsibility and performance, and we are determined to destroy this system under all conditions. [16: pg. 224-225]

Does this sound like fascism to you? Or maybe something like comrade Lenin, or campanero Castro, or, shall I dare say, socialist Bernie Sanders would say? But Hitler said it. In his own words he considered himself a socialist and anti-capitalist just like Marxism-Socialism advocates.

The above speech from Hitler is erroneously assigned to Gregor Strasser. Per the book "Hitler" by Joachim Fest, Hitler's speech was afterwards published in the Nazi Paper *Völkischer Beobachter* whose editor was Gregor Strasser, and therefore attributed to Gregor Strasser. The Marxist professors have gone out of their way to separate Hitler's National-Socialism from Marxist-Socialism. Some information on the Internet cannot be trusted due to zealous efforts of the Marxists to change the history per their ideology, as they always do, Hitler including.

However, what's more important to understand is what Hitler and the NAZI-Socialists did. This book will be an eye opener for anyone who's of the opinion that he was a fascist. Instead <u>Hitler was a first class Socialist</u>.

I realize that many people are sickened of learning what Hitler did, and others prohibit knowing anything about him, however, I found out that unlike the Marxists-Socialists who hide behind slogans while enslave nations, and kill anyone opposing them, Hitler was straight forward about what he did, how he did it, and why he undertook his National-Socialism revolution. Yes, his coming to power was a bloodless revolution, a Socialist revolution, and for that he is feared by the Marxist-Socialists. National-Socialism is the opponent to Marxism-Leninism-Communism-Socialism. If we don't learn from history, it is bound to repeat again in the future.

Fasten your seatbelts, folks, and learn who Hitler and the NAZI-Socialist party really were. By analyzing side by side Marxism-Socialism and National-Socialism you will see that they are identical, except for one point, which is misunderstood. Adolf Hitler was a monster and that will never change. But he was a *socialist* monster like the rest of them.

In another of his speeches Hitler said:
> The world is not here for a few people, and an order based eternally on the distinction between the haves and the have-nots does not exist anymore because the have-nots have determined to lay claim to their portion of God's earth. [4: Munich - April 12, 1922]

Hitler is allying with the have-nots to lay claim to their portion of earth. Fascists exploit the have-nots; they do not share the God's Earth with them. Only a Socialist would definitely do that.

The following is an extract from an interview with Adolf Hitler by George Sylvester Viereck, which took place in 1923, answering the question about socialism. It was republished in *Liberty* magazine in July 1932, and it appeared in *theguardian.com*:

> "Why," I asked Hitler, "do you call yourself a National Socialist, since your party programme is the very antithesis of that commonly accredited to socialism?"
>
> "Socialism," he retorted, putting down his cup of tea, pugnaciously, "is the science of dealing with the common weal. Communism is not Socialism. Marxism is not Socialism. The Marxians have stolen the term and confused its meaning. I shall take Socialism away from the Socialists.
>
> "Socialism is an ancient Aryan, Germanic institution. Marxism has no right to disguise itself as socialism. Socialism, unlike Marxism, does not repudiate private property. Unlike Marxism, it involves no negation of personality, and unlike Marxism, it is patriotic.
>
> "We chose to call ourselves the National Socialists. We are not internationalists. Our socialism is national." [14]

The interviewer was of the opinion that Marxism meant socialism, but Hitler considered true socialism his version of National-Socialism, and he definitely didn't want to be confused with Marxism. The world Marxist cause thinks Marxism is the only Socialist cause. In reality they both are socialist causes.

We were told that Adolf Hitler and the NAZIs were Fascist. And who told us that? Joseph Stalin, the mass murderer of the USSR. Why? It is on account of Benito Mussolini and his Italian Fascist Party, which successfully came to power in Italy, and in spite of the name, *Fascist*, the party was a Socialist party as well. Not all Socialist parties were Marxist-Leninist, and those other socialist parties Vladimir Ilych Lenin considered non-socialist because they were not controlled by Moscow. Therefore, in 1928 Joseph Stalin issued the order that only the Marxist-Leninist parties were *Socialists*, and everyone else was *Fascist*, as Mussolini's Fascist party was named.

And we *obeyed*.

Hitler's party was the NAZI party, or in German, NSDAP, National*sozialistische* Deutsche Arbeiterpartei. In English, NAZI means the National *Socialist* German *Workers'* Party. As a matter of fact, Hitler never called himself a fascist, but a *Nationalsozialistische*, a *National Socialist*. Yes, Hitler and the Nazis may have allied themselves with the likes of Italy's Fascist Mussolini and Spain's Falangist Franco governments, but Hitler and the NAZIs were not a fascist party, nor did they consider themselves fascists; just as the alliance between the United States and the Soviet Union during WW II did not make the United States a communist-socialist country.

OK, just because the words *Socialist* and *Workers* were included in the party's name that doesn't make NAZI or Hitler *Socialist*.

Maybe we need to understand what *Socialism* or *Socialist* really means.

Socialism can come in more convictions than Marxist-Socialism and Communist-Socialism. It can be Democratic-Socialism, Christian-Socialism, even feudal-socialism, agricultural-socialism, and bourgeois-socialism of the nineteenth century. In the evolution from feudalism into a new social order, the word *socialism* was used to represent the masses, the society's rise to power.

According to F. Engels, [1] *The Communist Manifesto* was not called *The Socialist Manifesto* because in 1847 Socialism signified the bourgeois and other movements, whereas Communism signified working-class movements. But since then, all socialist movements have been identified mistakenly as Marxism-Socialism, and since the collapse of the communist economic systems and the discrediting of Communism, the leftists have renamed themselves as Socialists, Marxists, Leftists, Liberals, or Progressives.

Socialism is the same horror house under a new name and management.

The socialism known today is based on *The Communist Manifesto* by Karl Marx and Friedrich Engels, published in 1848, which was a turbulent revolutionary year.

Regardless of what type of *socialism* we discuss, all types of socialism have one thing in common: They try to benefit their society through a unified dogma applicable to all members without any deviation or reinterpretation, meaning that society's rule is imposed on all individuals of that society with no exception. Individual freedom is subservient to the common cause of socialism or the community.

Communism is guided by Marxist-Leninist rules, and at its core is the immutable principle that the state in the name of society owns all the wealth of the nation for the common good of all, and *no individual* can enrich himself/herself from or profit through another man's work, asset, capital, mineral rights, land, inheritance, or anything that will make that individual *rich*, in other words, *not needing to work*.

The Marxist-Socialists object to calling Hitler a Socialist because he never confiscated the wealth of the rich. For pragmatic reasons, as you will see, Hitler chose to let the economy remain in the hands of the capitalists, and allow them to keep their assets and even prosper. It is true, Hitler did not confiscate the wealth of his nation's rich.
<u>However,</u>
he planned on confiscating other nation's wealth; that of the USSR.

All socialist regimes have an inherent inability to stay in power in a country unless they have dictatorial powers, and they will kill to maintain the absolute power they have to enforce their socialist principles.

From *How Socialist Was Adolf Hitler?*:

> Professor Stackelberg also makes it plain in his work that he considers the Left to be the "progressive" end, and although he accepts that at the extreme ends of the spectrum there will be "movements who will go to any lengths to achieve their utopian ideal... [8]

Yes, be that the Marxist-Socialists, the Marxist-Leninists, or National-Socialists they will go to any lengths, including murdering hundreds of millions of people to achieve their socialist ideal.

Totalitarian Socialism of any kind—Communist-Socialist or National-Socialist—is, as you'll see, the biggest killer in human history.

Chapter 2. Socialism Kills

The atrocities committed by Hitler and his party *would never have been committed by good socialists*. Really? Like the *good socialists* of the rest of the world? Let's see what history tells us about the *Good Socialists*:

☭ The good Communist-Socialist Mao Tse-tung killed one hundred million—100,000,000—of his people.

☭ The good Communist-Socialist Joseph Stalin, and his predecessors Lenin and Trotsky, killed a mere fifty million—50,000,000—of his people.

☭ The good Communist-Socialist Pol Pot, killed only two million—2,000,000—Cambodian people out of a population of eight million in just four years.

☭ The good Communist-Socialist comrades from the rest of the world like Ho Shi Minh (one million deaths) in Viet Nam, Fidel Castro (unknown deaths) in Cuba, Kim dictators (two million deaths and counting) in North Korea, Nicolae Ceausescu and his predecessor Gheorghe Gheorghiu Dej, (three hundred thousand deaths) in Romania, or all other *good* Communist-Socialists in East Germany, Poland, Czechoslovakia, Hungary, Albania, and Bulgaria who killed more millions of their citizens. Let's not forget the millions killed by the Marxist-Socialist governments in Africa and Latin America. Altogether, the above-mentioned socialist states'

killings could amount to more than twenty million —
20,000,000 — deaths.

Like all the other socialists, Hitler killed eleven
million — 11,000,000 — people, half of them Jews and the
other half political prisoners, the infirm, the racially unfit,
and other ethnic groups like the gypsies.

*These morbid numbers represent Socialism and its
"greatest" leaders.*

Wait! Those killings were committed by Communists!
Well, Communism is Marxism-Leninism. Socialism is a
transient form of government. If it exists in a democratic
country it does not have complete power of the
government. The moment it starts implementing the 10
Rules of the Communist Manifesto, they will be voted out
of power or a civil war will start and in order to survive the
Socialists will have to win by killing and install itself as a
totalitarian government, a Communist Government.

War casualties are not included in the above casualties.
The figures shown above are taken from a variety of
sources, such as *The Black Book of Communism: Crimes,
Terror and Repression*, or the topic of "Mass killings
under communist regimes" in Wikipedia, and other old
resources that have vanished from the internet. Not
surprisingly considering Google's leftist agenda. The
figures vary widely as many of these killings were never
properly recorded or the information was destroyed. Some
critics, no doubt Marxists-Socialists, argue that famine
should not be counted in the total number of killings.
Regardless, if the governments used famine as a weapon,
which they did, or the government policies caused the
famines as in the USSR, China, and Africa, the deaths

18

were caused by Socialism. The Marxist-Socialists and their adherents in the online media try to lower the death figures to minimize their atrocities, just like the white supremacists and the Muslims deny the Holocaust ever happened. Who knows? One day we might find mass graves in China and Siberia revealing mind-boggling atrocities committed by the Communist-Socialists.

Don't excuse socialism and blame only the individual leaders. Socialism and any totalitarian political system are the breeding grounds for such brutes, who surface and metastasize into monsters without exception. And mass killers like Hitler, Stalin, and Mao would not have committed their atrocities without help from the entire political system.

Yes, but did Hitler, Mao, or Stalin line up that many people against a wall and shoot them, or gas them? Many of them *were* executed by shooting. Stalin, while transporting the condemned for execution, used exhaust gas from trucks to kill them, just like Hitler.

In the words of *The Black Book of Communism*, people were killed in many ways:

> The pattern includes execution by various means, such as firing squads, hanging, drowning, battering, and in certain cases gassing, poisoning, or "Car accidents"; destruction of population by starvation, through man-made famine, the withholding of food or both; deportation, through which death can occur in transit (either through physical exhaustion, or through confinement in an enclosed space), at one's place of residence, or

through forced labor (exhaustion, illness, hunger, cold). [9: pg 4]

And this unimaginable killing was done over a span of many years, even decades. Hitler was in charge for twelve years. Mao's terror reign was twenty-six years. And Lenin-Stalin's terror reign lasted thirty-six years.

Only Pol Pot, of the Khmer Rouge, is in a class by himself. He deliberately murdered his population over a period of four years. After his thugs rounded up the suspects; took them to detention centers, which in many cases were high school buildings; tortured them to confess their crimes and divulge the names of other associates, they were condemned to immediate execution. Every night the condemned were taken by truckloads to the "killing fields" for execution and burial in mass graves. Most were killed by hitting them on the head with a stick that had a nail protruding from it, after which they were pushed into a previously dug mass grave and buried, even if many of them were not yet dead. Mothers with young children were killed as well, but only after their children were swung by the feet to crush their skulls against the trunks of trees nearby. Imagine the horror at these sites, as Khmer Rouge Socialist propaganda music played from loudspeakers to mask the screams of the victims.

Bulldozers filled the mass graves covering the convulsing bodies, after which they dug fresh mass graves for the next night's massacre. In the meantime, Pol Pot's soldiers rounded up new suspects, and the process repeated day and night. I gathered this information personally at one of the killing fields when I visited Cambodia.

Hitler Was a Socialists

But only Hitler specifically killed the Jews, 5,500,000 of them, because of their ethnicity and religion. We should not put him in the same socialist basket as the Marxist-Socialists. True and appalling about killing the Jews, especially after seeing the pictures of the concentration camps, the corpses in pictures, or visiting the NAZI industrial extermination camps. Unfortunately, we don't have pictures to document exterminations at Soviet gulags or Chinese concentration camps. The Soviets and the Chinese were not defeated in war and caught bloody handed, exposing their extermination camps and the millions of corpses they disposed of. Soviet camps have long disappeared, while the Chinese camps are thriving as the Chinese Communist Party will never run out of enemies, real or imaginary.

Stalin starved to death up to 11,000,000 Ukrainians because they opposed him and because they were Ukrainians. In the purges of 1936–38, he also killed untold numbers of Soviet-Polish citizens because they were Polish. Do you think the Jews in the Soviet Union were treated humanely? Only in the pro-socialist movies. Under Stalin they were tolerated as a necessary nuisance.

The following is an excerpt from an article "Vladimir Lenin Was Part Jewish, Say Declassified KGB Files" suggesting what was in store for the Jews under Stalin:

> This fascinating morsel of information, gleaned from declassified KGB files, is not a minor detail in a country where anti-Semitism was a recognized state doctrine for decades. Starting in the 1930s, the Soviet regime—spurred on by its leader Joseph Stalin—launched a violent discriminatory campaign against Jewish citizens.

> A few years later, Stalin began to purge Jews
> from among the leaders of the revolution. Prior
> to his death in 1953, furthermore, he was
> preparing to send the whole Jewish population
> living in the Soviet Union to concentration
> camps in Siberia. [15]

That was the thank-you Stalin gave to the Jews after they
had spied for him and had given him the American
nuclear-bomb secrets.

After invading Poland in 1939, Stalin had 22,000 Polish
military officers, police officers, and intelligentsia shot in
the Katyn Forest, just because they were Polish, not to
mention the ethnic cleansing Stalin imposed in the newly
acquired territories of Moldova, Bessarabia, the Baltic
States and many other such regions. Millions of ethnic
Romanians were removed from their homes in Bessarabia
and Moldova and relocated to Siberia, after which the
Romanian homes were repopulated by Russians. The
process was called *Russification*. The Romanians sent to
Siberia were lucky if they survived and were able to tell
their horrific stories decades later. The same thing
happened in Ukraine. Why do you think that there are so
many Russians living in East Ukraine and that this region
wants to secede from Ukraine and join Russia? The list
goes on to include millions of others, like Cossacks,
Chechens, Russian-Germans, Tatars, and probably just
about any ethnic group in the Soviet Union. How many
died during relocation or were killed by famine and harsh
weather in Siberia? We may never know.

Continuing the theme of genocide, must it refer to just a
racial or ethnic group? How about an entire *social class* of
people? The bourgeois, the rich? It didn't matter if you

built your wealth with your own hands, sacrificed, and lived frugally, as it happened to my maternal family; all it took to be executed or sent to the gulag was the fact that you possessed wealth.

The following was the thought among Bolsheviks at the end of 1918, expressed by one of their political police officers, Latvian M. Latsis, a member of Cheka, the Soviet secret police:

> We don't make war against any people in particular. *We are exterminating the bourgeoisie as a class*. In your investigation don't look for documents and pieces of evidence about what the defendant has done, whether in deed or in speaking or acting against Soviet authority. The first question you should ask him is what class he comes from, what are his roots, his education, his training, and his occupation. [9: pg 8] (Emphasis added.)

The class a person belonged to, determined the fate of that individual. Indeed, this is what the Bolshevik Red Terror, when people were executed for who they were not for what they did, was all about. Just like the Jews in Germany. That's why the Communist-Socialists killed so many millions of people. Based on Marxist-Leninist principles, it was extermination of an entire class of people.

And to make sure that the killing went on unabated, consider the following from *The Black Book of Communism*:

> From the end of the 1920s, the State Political Directorate (GPU, the new name for Cheka) introduced a quota method – each region and district had to arrest, deport, or shoot a certain

> percentage of people who were members of
> several "enemy" social classes. [9: pg 15]

The only other time in history when an entire class of people was killed was during the French Revolution when aristocrats and clergy were sent to the guillotine.

The crime of *genocide* has been expanded as a crime against humanity to include, as the French Criminal code states:

> *The deed of executing a concerted effort* that
> strives to destroy totally or partially a national,
> ethnic, racial or religious group, or a group that
> has been determined on the basis of any other
> *arbitrary criterion.* [9: pg 8] Emphasis added.

But who cares if the Communist-Socialists killed the filthy rich, the exploiters and thieves of the upper classes? Aren't the Jews portrayed in the same way? It makes no difference why you exterminate a class or race or people. They are all people.

But not all people are counted the same, as we are told in literature and movies, and the NAZI-Socialists are villainized more than the Communist-Socialists, who killed more people by far. There seems to be only so much hatred that the people can accept from any of those killers.

The Black Book of Communism says:

> For Nazism's unique status as "absolute evil"
> is now so entrenched that any comparison with
> it easily appears suspect.
> Of the several reasons for this assessment of
> Nazism, the most obvious is that the Western
> Democracies fought the World War II in a kind
> of global "popular front" against "fascism."

> The ultimate distinguishing characteristic of Nazism, of course, is the Holocaust, considered as the historically unique crime of seeking the extermination of an entire people, crime for which the term "genocide" was coined. . ... And therewith the Jewish people acquired the solemn obligation to keep the memory of its martyrs alive in the conscience of the world. [9: pg xii]

The Jews have done an outstanding job at keeping the genocide alive in our minds, and should continue to do so. But Hollywood is predominantly Jewish and leftist and has accomplished two goals with the anti-NAZI movies: They remind us about the Holocaust, which must be remembered, but also cause us to ignore the atrocities against humanity that the Communist-Socialists have committed—and that is inexcusable.

From the *The Black Book of Communism*:

> Hitler and Nazism are now a constant presence in Western print and on Western television, whereas Stalin [or Mao] and Communism materialize only sporadically. The status of ex-Communist carries with it no stigma, even when unaccompanied by any expression of regret; past contact with Nazism, however, no matter how marginal or remote, confers an indelible stain. [9: pg xiii]

In this book you'll learn that the Devil is the same, and its name is Socialism. We must remember the hundreds of millions of other people killed by Communist-Socialists along with NAZI-Socialists. Killing is killing. For every one Jew killed by Hitler, thirty-five other people— Russians, Ukrainians, Poles, Germans, Romanians, Hungarians, Bulgarians, Chinese, Vietnamese, Cubans,

Africans, Nicaraguans, and Venezuelans among many others—were killed by the Communism-Socialism, *a thirty-five to one ratio.*

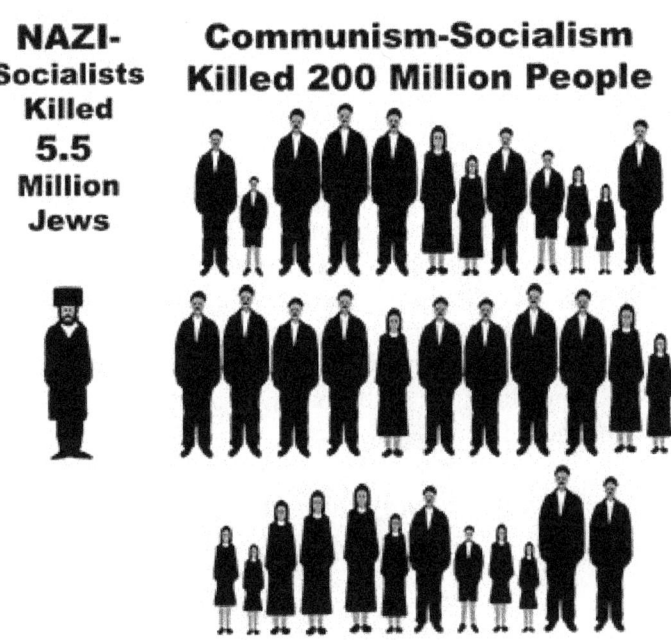

NAZI-Socialists Killed 5.5 Million Jews

Communism-Socialism Killed 200 Million People

For every one Jew killed by NAZI-Socialism 35 more people of all ethnicities, ages, or sexes were killed by Communism-Socialism.

Who is mourning and remember these people?

Where is the monument in their memory showing the atrocities committed by the Communism-Socialism? There is none.

You may wonder why I mentioned Africa as being included in the killings by Socialism.

This is what was said in *The Black Book of Communism*:

> One particular feature of Communist regimes—their systematic use of famine as a weapon.
>
> This policy was a recipe for creating famine on a massive scale. Remember in the period after 1918, only Communist countries experienced such famines, which led to the deaths of hundreds of thousands, and in some cases millions, of people. And again, in the 1980s, two African countries that claimed to be Marxist-Leninist, Ethiopia and Mozambique, were the only such countries to suffer these deadly famines. [9: pg 9]

Socialism in any form kills with impunity.

Chapter 3. Hitler Was Not a Fascist

But NAZI-Socialism is considered a fascist political party. How do they get the name fascist? As mentioned earlier and according to Wikipedia:

> At its 6th Congress in July 1928, Stalin informed delegates that the main threat to socialism came not from the Right but from non-Marxist socialists and social democrats, whom he called "social fascists"; Stalin recognized that in many countries, the social democrats were the Marxist-Leninists' main rivals for working-class support.

Even before this declaration in 1928, Lenin considered all other Marxist-Socialist parties not under the control of Moscow, throughout the world as the enemy, and the only ones to be defined as true socialists were the Bolsheviks, or Marxist-Leninists. Later, the word *fascism* was applied to all the other socialist parties, taking after Benito Mussolini's Fascist party.

What did Benito Mussolini's Fascist party do to deserve such *fame*? In his younger years, Mussolini was a member of the Italian Socialist Party, a Marxist-Socialist party, and the editor of their magazine, *Avanti!* In 1914 he was ousted from the Italian Socialist Party because of his nationalistic views. Marxism-Socialism is an *internationalist* movement; he was a nationalist. He joined the Fasces of Revolutionary Action and later the Italian Fasces of Combat, both National-Socialist movements. Fasces, in

Imperial Rome, represented the image of a bundle of sticks surrounding an axe, symbolizing power and authority. Mussolini founded the National Fascist Party (Partito Nazionale Fascista or PNF) in 1921, and the name *fascist, fascista,* was used for his party. Mussolini never stopped being a socialist, and he maintained his beliefs that nationalism and socialism combine to create a potent political movement. In 1922, Mussolini and his National Fascist Party initiated the March on Rome and took over the Italian government in a bloodless coup d'état. Italy became a Fascist state, or, more accurately, a National-Socialist state.

At this point, the big rift occurred between the Marxists-Leninists and all the other Marxists and Socialist movements. The Bolshevik revolution was the first time a Marxist-Socialist party took power in a country. But in 1922 in Italy, another Socialist party, the National Fascist Party, took over the power in another country, representing a major competition for the Marxist-Leninists in their ambition to take over the world.

Lenin decreed that a Marxism-Leninism government is a *dictatorship of the proletariat,* bent on destroying all private wealth and on the elimination of bourgeois exploitation and of the bourgeoisie as a class. Mussolini's Fascist (Socialist) party was also a totalitarian government, but it was a *dictatorship of all people,* not only of the proletariat, for the benefit of all people. Marxism-Socialism is based on class conflict, antagonistic toward the bourgeoisie, the industrialists, and the church. The Italian Fascist (Socialist) party was based on revolutionary nationalism, or a people's nation unified by the community for the common good. It meant being friendlier toward the industrialists and sharing the wealth with the rest of the nation's people.

What's worse is that Marxism-Leninism acquires power by force, through bloody revolution. The Italian Fascist (Socialist) party acquired power through a bloodless coup d'état because it was a popular movement. Later on, in 1933, the NAZI-Socialist party was voted into power by the German people. This difference about how you get to power and how you treat the wealthy class is what caused the Marxist-Socialists to exclude the Italian Fascist and National-Socialist parties from being called Socialists. In other words, *you are a socialist only if you kill the wealthy class and get political power through bloodshed.* Hitler and Mussolini did none of those things, and they don't deserve the *prestige* of being called *socialists*. To differentiate between the two causes, Stalin decreed all the other Socialist parties *Fascist.* If Hitler had come to power before Mussolini, most likely *Nazism* would have been the name given to all other socialist causes.

But this difference in the confiscation of property between the two socialist systems seems to justify the name fascist for Hitler and Mussolini. But, that's false. Fascism is a dictatorship representing the rule of the oligarchy; socialism is a dictatorship representing the rule of the society and their self-appointed leaders. As you'll see soon, regardless of the two approaches, both political causes were based on socialism and intended to benefit the people of that country by making radical socioeconomic changes. Again, Fascism is for the benefit of the oligarchy, not the people.

Francisco Franco's Falangists in Spain were the real fascists. They established a political and economic system protecting the monarchy, capitalists, landowners, nobility, and the church. (The Spanish king was sent into exile by the republicans/Marxists.) It was a nationalistic party as well, on the right wing of the political spectrum. Since that time, the political spectrum has been divided between Marxism and Fascism, left and right, rather than between Socialism, Freedom, and Fascism (Not NAZI or Italian fascista.)

As far as Hitler was concerned, the takeover of the German government by the NAZI-Socialists was a socialist revolution.

Berlin, Reichstag–Speech of January 30, 1937, Hitler said:

> They speak of democracies and dictatorships, and have not realized that in this country a Revolution has taken place that can be described as democratic in the highest sense of the word. Does a more glorious socialism or a truer democracy exist than that which enables any German boy to find his way to the head of the nation? The purpose of the revolution was not to deprive a privileged class of its rights, but to raise a class without rights to equality. [4: Berlin, Reichstag–Speech of January 30, 1937]

Hitler considered Nationalist-Socialist democracy superior to capitalist democracy and intended to raise everyone's prosperity and opportunities.

But then why is the whole world accepting the lie that NAZI was Fascism? Two reasons:

First, Hitler is the focus of all the hatred in this world. He is Satan. Because he lost the war and he was caught with hands bloodied by the people he exterminated, we found out what monsters he and the NAZI-Socialists were. To associate the world hatred for what he did with socialism would be terminal for any socialistic cause. Even with all the eyewitnesses who experienced the horror of Communism-Socialism, it is easy to sweep under the rug the *alleged* atrocities committed by them compared to the proof we have of Hitler's atrocities.

Second, labeling Hitler and Nazism as Fascism and on the right of the political spectrum, of the rich, of the discriminatory and racist nationalists, funnels all the hatred toward the right and diverts the focus from what the Communist-Socialists did and what the new socialists are capable of doing now and in the future. As you'll see throughout this book, by comparing NAZI-Socialism words and deeds with Marxist-Socialism words and deeds, you'll realize that they all are socialists and all capable of committing the most horrendous atrocities.

According to Wikipedia, the modern definition of Fascism is as follows:

> **Fascism** is a form of radical right-wing, authoritarian, ultranationalism characterized by dictatorial power, forcible suppression of opposition, and strong regimentation of society and of the economy which came to prominence in early 20th-century Europe.

This is one definition for fascism tailored to Mussolini's fascist party. Also, as I mentioned earlier, Fascism was not new in the twentieth century. It existed with many other names: monarchy, the feudal system, imperialism, and colonialism. The definition includes the word *ultranationalism*, not nationalism, so that it won't be confused with other Nationalist-Socialist parties which exist today around the world.

Ultranationalism is not a proprietary feature of Fascism, as all Communist-Socialist governments, in practice, were as *ultranationalist* as the NAZI were. If ultranationalism or nationalism were the sole criteria of fascism, all nations on earth should be fascist. And the Olympics could be described as a *fascist festivity*. Aren't all the athletes marching under their countries' flags? Aren't they competing for the honor of their nations? Don't the medal counts give status to the countries that have won the most? Aren't the national anthems played for the winners' countries? Nationalism is not a bad word, although the Marxist-Socialist world movement wants to make it such because of National-Socialism.

If National-Socialism was a fascist party, Mexico, our southern neighbor, and the PRI (Partido Revolucionario Institucional) government would be a NAZI/fascist country, because, to be sure, Mexico is a National-Socialist country, and the PRI controlled Mexico continuously for seventy-one years. Have you heard the slogan *Mexico for Mexicans*? The Mexicans in the United States, even if they are US citizens, proudly display the Mexican flag over the American flag. A foreigner cannot buy property in Mexico, although some restrictions have been loosened recently to foster prosperity and attract foreign investment. The same fact would apply to all former European communist countries, which did not permit any foreign country or citizen to own any land or businesses in those countries.

Neither nationalism nor ultranationalism is a prerequisite for fascism.

My definition for Fascism is:

> **Fascism** is as a right-wing political and economic system protecting the oligarchy, the establishment, monarchy, nobility, military, monopolists, landowners, social strata, and the church, and ignoring the people.

This definition does not match the "official definition" of fascism, but, in my opinion, it is more accurate, reflecting the difference between haves and have-nots. In modern days the nobility has disappeared. The power of the church has diminished substantially since the mid-twentieth century and could no longer be considered part of the oligarchy. Better yet, the "church" in most cases has moved to the left to maintain popular support. In the past, God would reward the people in the afterlife if they behaved. Today people want the rewards in this life.

All authoritarian monarchies were fascist in nature, just like any other non-socialist or military dictatorship is fascist. In Fascism, the laborers/proletariat/people are not included in the power structure. This brings up a shocking observation: What is China today? If you say Communist-Socialist, that's what it used to be. As a matter of fact, China has been a National-Socialist (NAZI) country ever since it allowed private ownership of businesses and profit to be part of its economy. The Communist Party, its members, and the new self-made billionaires are the oligarchy. People don't select their leaders; the establishment selects the leaders for the sole benefit of their own totalitarian clique and state monopolies.

To be sure, Fascism is not the government for the people, and Hitler never called himself or the NAZI party a fascist party. Instead it was a National-Socialist party, and his actions were based on socialist principles.

Fascism is the dictatorship of the oligarchy.

Chapter 4. What Is Socialism?

Today, socialism is commonly misunderstood as Marxism. Socialism according to Wikipedia is as follows:

Socialism is a range of economic and social systems characterized by social ownership of the means of production and workers' self-management, as well as the political theories and movements associated with them. Social ownership can be public, collective or cooperative ownership, or citizen ownership of equity. *There are many varieties of socialism* and there is no single definition encapsulating all of them, with social ownership being the common element shared by its various forms. . . . Socialist politics has been both *internationalist and nationalist* in orientation.

The emphasis is mine to point out that socialism can exist in many forms, including the nationalist form, just like National-Socialism. The Wikipedia definition continues:

By the late 19th century, after the work of Karl Marx and his collaborator Friedrich Engels, socialism had come to signify opposition to capitalism and advocacy for a post-capitalist system based on some form of social ownership of the means of production.

As of the twenty-first century, the power of monarchy, nobility, and the church have diminished or all but died away, with the exception of some countries in Asia and the Muslim world. Democracy, capitalism, and military dictatorship are the new enemies of socialism. Capitalism can thrive under both democracy and fascism, but never under socialism.

Under socialism, all economic and political power is in the hands or supervision of the socialist state for the "betterment" of the proletariat/workers. In socialism, the workers/people—the have-nots—are the supposed power and the state becomes the dictatorship of the proletariat, as Lenin said. And the elimination of classes was mandatory; there were no more exploiters and exploited.

A note about the difference between Socialism and Communism. Socialism is based on Karl Marx's book *The Communist Manifesto*, and the so-called communist countries were called communist because of the ruling party, the Communist Party. Those countries never achieved communism, only socialism. Communism can be achieved only after implementing socialism, which always fails. Then what is communism? Under communism the money or possessions will not exist. Every person will work for the benefit of the *commune* of people without pay. In return the people are entitled to use the goods and benefits of their work without payment. Communism is based on what Carl Marx said:

> From each according to his abilities, to each according to his needs.

Everyone has needs, but not everyone is willing to work for them. In other words, welfare for all without money.

Hitler said in another of his speeches:

> And finally they all fail to understand that we must on *principle free ourselves from any class standpoint. . ...* They should learn that in a single State there is only one supreme citizen—right, one supreme citizen—honor, and that is the right and honor of honest work. They should further learn that the *social* idea must be the essential foundation for any State, otherwise no

> state can permanently endure . . . it can prevail only if
> what it seeks to restore does truly correspond to *the*
> *welfare of a whole people.* [4: Munich Speech April 12, 1922]
> Emphasis added.

Hitler clearly states that socialistic ideas must be the foundation of any socialistic state, such as the government that his party, the National Socialist party, will form. Fascism would never care about the "welfare of a whole people" or freeing "ourselves from any class standpoint."

What the definition from Wikipedia failed to mention is that socialism eliminates the class system. All people are equal without differentiation by social status, and like a diligent socialist, Hitler fulfilled that promise.

To exemplify how deeply ingrained socialism was in the higher echelons of the NAZI party, Joachim Fest tells us that:

> Goebbels spoke with deep respect of the Russian utopian impulse, while Strasser even called for an alliance with Moscow "against the militarism of France, against the imperialism of England, against the capitalism of Wall Street." [2]

And Goebbels added:

> It would be better for us to end our existence under Bolshevism than to endure slavery under capitalism. I think it is terrible that we [the Nazis] and the Communists are bashing in each other's heads. . .. Where can we get together sometime with the leading Communists? [3: pg 126]

Goebbels, Hitler's minister of propaganda, and Gregor Strasser, second in command until Hitler killed him in 1934, were true believers in Marxism-Socialism during their ascent to power. Hitler and the NAZI party followed the Marxist principles. Hitler even admitted of Marxism:

> I have learned a great deal from Marxism. I admit that without hesitation. Not from that boring social theory

and materialist conception of history, not at all from that absurd nonsense. . ... But I've learned from their methods. [2: p126]

Hitler plainly recognized that National-Socialism was a carbon copy of Marxism, but without "boring social theory and materialist conception of history," in other words, without their doctrine against materialism.

From the book *How Socialist Was Adolf Hitler?* by Alan Brown, comes the following information:

Roderick Stackelberg called Nazism a "radical variant of fascism," but in placing it firmly on the right of the political spectrum he makes the same error as many other historians but using Marxist socialism as his benchmark. Furthermore, his interpretations are value-loaded as the extract below clearly demonstrates:

The essential difference between left and right lies in their attitude toward human equality as a social ideal. *The more a person deems absolute equality among all the people to be a desirable condition, the further to the Left [he] or she will be. . . .* The more a person considers inequality to be unavoidable or even desirable, the further to the Right he or she will be. [8]
[19: pg 4]

I emphasized the above sentence about *equality*. The NAZI-Socialists were all for equality of all the German people. Hitler never considered inequality to be unavoidable or even desirable; that was not what Hitler stood for.

It is completely erroneous to consider only the Marxist-Leninist cause to the Left and everyone else, including other branches of socialism, to the Right. Considering that

Nationalism and Marxism are both socialist causes, the political spectrum should be based on Socialism/Oppression–Democracy/Freedom–Fascism/Oppression, as shown below:

Socialism Oppression	Democracy Freedom	Fascism Oppression
Marxism-Socialism	Democracy	Fascism (not NAZI)
Communist-Socialism		Military-Dictatorship
National-Socialism		Theocracy
X, Y, Z – Socialism		Monarchy (absolute)

Besides Joseph Stalin declaring all socialist parties as fascists and of the right, in *How Socialist Was Adolf Hitler?* Alan Brown gives us the following information:

> George Watson notes that early socialist commentators did not perceive Hitlerism as "right wing," and that the distinction only emerged during the Spanish Civil War, which placed Hitler and Stalin on opposite sides, hence Left and Right "on grounds of argumentative convenience" like "cops and robbers, cowboys and Indians."
>
> John Ray argued that Nazism and fascism are generally placed on the Right only in relation to communism because that is the "dominant perspective of intellectuals in most of the 20th century."
>
> Watson suggests that Hitler would not have understood the "Left versus the Right"

argument at all, and perhaps would have seen no point to "a linear theory of politics." [8]

Marxism-Socialism's purpose is allegedly to serve the proletariat, the factory worker, as was envisioned by Lenin. But if you are an agricultural worker, a tradesman, a craftsman, a member of the bourgeoisie, a landowner, clergy, or a member of any other occupation, you'd be ruled only by the proletariat dictatorship. They are one of the many after all. What makes them so special? It is their concentration and ability to organize, following a Marxist-Socialist fanatic to obtain total political and economic power. [8]

Marxism-Socialism relies on three principles:

- *Totalitarianism*
- *Elimination of personal freedom*
- *Elimination of private property and profit/wealth.*

Because National Socialism did not nationalize the wealth of the rich and eliminate profit, the diehard socialists declared that National-Socialism was socialist only in name. Hitler had only to look at the Soviet Union to see what a disaster that economy was after their nationalization. Under National-Socialism, the belief was that all people deserved riches for their labor, not just the already rich. But Marxism-Socialism destroys wealth to achieve economic equality among the people. National-Socialism wants to acquire additional wealth by invading other countries to improve the German people's wealth. (Or, in the case of Mexico, to prevent foreigners from *exploiting* the Mexicans.) Not nationalizing the German economy was done for practical purposes, which will be addressed later.

Hitler did not hesitate to demonize the rich people and the capitalists, especially if their money was made from speculation and not earned like that of decent working people. This strategy worked well, and he enlarged the National-Socialist appeal to the masses.

Hitler expressed the following:

> So is the worker, producing in shops and factories for a pittance, while the shareholder draws dividends and bonuses which he has not worked for. So is the earning middle class, whose work goes almost entirely to pay the interest on bank overdrafts. So are all who must earn their bread by mental or bodily work, while a comparatively small portion, without labor or trouble, pocket huge profits out of their dividends, speculations and bank shares. [6: pg 36]

This is in full concordance with *Communist Manifesto* rule 1 and 8.

Bernie Sanders commented along the same lines:

> Democratic socialism means that we must create an economy that works for all, not just the very wealthy.

Funny! Isn't this the way democrat Michael Bloomberg made his money? Through speculation in the stock market. Hitler, the socialist, was against these ill-gotten gains.

Socialism can come to power by force/revolution, by coup-d'état, by fraudulent elections, or, on rare occasions, by free democratic elections. Adolph Hitler and the National-Socialist party had first tried to take over the

Bavarian government in 1923 in their famous *Putsch*—and failed. After Hitler was released from prison, he revived the National-Socialist party, and its representatives were first elected to the Reichstag in 1928. Just five years later, in 1933, the NAZI-Socialists were elected democratically as the largest block in Reichstag, and came to dominate Germany soon after.

The table below presents the political, economic, and social similarities and differences between Fascism, Nazism, Socialism, and Communism:

Institutions	Fascism*	NAZI-Socialism	Democratic-Socialism**	Communism***
Government	Totalitarian	Totalitarian	Totalitarian	Totalitarian
Big business	Pro	Control	Control	State Owned
Small business	Pro	Pro	Pro	State Owned
Big church	Pro	Control	Control	Abolish
Big landowners	Pro	Control	Control	State Owned
Small landowners	Pro	Pro	Pro	State Owned
Media	Control	Control	Control	State Owned
Nationalism	Pro	Pro	Pro	Pro
Internationalism	Against	Against	Pro	Pro
Intelligentsia	Control	Control	Control	Control
Proletariat Peasants	Against	Pro	Pro	Pro-Controlled
Other Political Parties	Right Wing only	One Party	Leftist and center parties are tolerated	One Party
Freedom of Expression	No	Limited-Censored	Limited-Censored	No
Freedom of Movement	Pro	Pro	Pro	No
Labor Unions	Against	Control	Control	State Owned
Personal Freedom	No	No	Limited	No
Police ****	Protects the Government	Protects the People	Protects the People	Protects the Government

*Fascism indicated here represents the type of Fascism in Franco's Spain.

**Democratic-Socialism is of the Marxist belief. In its pure form, it is a transitional political system. In many cases, it resembles a democratic system; however, because of its underlying Marxist principles and inefficiencies, the economy will decline. If elections are allowed, it will be voted out of power or replaced through fraudulent elections by communism.

***Communism is Marxist-Leninism that evolved from Marxism.

**** Police are government institutions, but as such the political party in charge has a great effect on the police actions. Police in this case does not mean Gestapo, which was a political secret service, like the Stasi in East Germany or KGB in the USSR.

Out of seventeen points, NAZI-Socialism matches Democratic (Marxist)-Socialism on fourteen points. On the other hand, Fascism and National Socialism match only on ten out of seventeen points.

The only organization that all these regimes have in common is the military, which belongs to the state and was omitted from the table.

Socialism has proven many times that it is an expansionary political system. The USSR occupied and converted the Central European countries to socialism. It invaded Hungary in 1956 to end the freedom revolution there, and Warsaw Pact military invaded Czechoslovakia in 1968 for the same reason. In 1969, there was a military conflict between the Communist USSR and Communist China. The Soviet Union invaded Afghanistan in 1979. And it exported its socialist philosophy all over the world, causing more wars, famine, and deaths. Cuba intervened militarily or politically in Angola, Equatorial Guinea, Ethiopia, Guinea-Bissau, Grenada, Mozambique, Nicaragua, and Venezuela.

Defining Adolf Hitler and his NAZI party as socialists doesn't change the fact that World War II was fought and that millions of people lost their lives. The horror of that war will not change, but understanding who or what political system of government was responsible is crucial. The point is that the evil of War World II was perpetuated by *two forms of socialism*—NAZI-Socialism and Communist-Socialism—and socialism was therefore responsible for all atrocities in Europe.

There should be no doubt that the United States did not defeat Fascism in World War II, but another form of Socialism, NAZI-Socialism.

Chapter 5. What's the Point?

Who am I to make such an outrageous declaration that Adolf Hitler was a socialist and not a fascist? I'm not an academician, most of whom are leftists or Marxists who wouldn't dare to utter such blasphemous words—if they value their careers, or want to maintain their good status in the American Socialist or Communist Parties. Therefore, this book is written without Leftists bias, or for that matter a Rightist bias. But because I lived under the socialist hell, the book has an anti-socialist bias. I consider Marxism-Socialism to be the most tyrannical form of political government devised by men.

I consider myself an educated man, but not an intellectual. I did meaningful work in my life; I do not theorize in utopia. I have a Bachelor of Science in Engineering and Industrial Management, and I am a student of history. I published fifteen other books, mostly fantasy and science-fiction and one non-fiction book, *Escape from Communism*, [7] about my escape from Communist-Socialist Romania.

I was born and grew up under Communist-Socialism, and when I was eighteen years old, I escaped from the Communist *hell*. When I say escape, that means literally *escape*. Most communist countries and definitely the Socialist Republic of Romania resembled concentration camps. The border had tall walls, even taller watch towers, barbed wire fences, ditches, border patrols with guns ready to shoot, and dogs to chase any desperado who might try to get out of the "proletariat paradise." All these measures were taken to keep the people in, not the enemy or illegal aliens out.

I wrote my horrifying story in the book *Escape from Communism*. [7]

I highly recommend you read it to understand what life was all about under such a brutal political system and what unimaginable atrocities were committed against the citizens by the Communist-Socialist party in order to maintain its power. The book also contains my explanation of the Communist-Socialist political system and why it can never possibly work, although until Marxism-Leninism disappears from this world, it will destroy more millions of lives. In my book, I give an example of what would happen if the United States became a socialist country. I think it is a good economic reference for how disastrous socialism is and what to expect.

I know and experienced socialism firsthand when I lived in the Socialist Republic of Romania. I consider myself a knowledgeable person when it comes to the practical application and operation of socialism. I, like many other people, thought that socialism meant Marxism, until one day I watched *Hitler's Empire: The Post-War Plan,* produced by AHC, which analyzed what Hitler did during the years between his election and the start of World War II. I knew that Hitler's NAZI government resurrected Germany's economy after its loss in the Great War and its fall into the grips of the Great Depression, but not much else. Most of my knowledge was about the war.

What piqued my interest, while watching the episode "Hitler's Empire: The Post-War Plan," was that the NAZIs built resorts on the Baltic Sea, the Colossus of Prora at

Ruegen, a 4.5 km (2.8mi) long building, housing 20,000 guests per week for the benefit of the German workers' relaxation and enjoyment. Fascist governments don't build resorts for their people. However, Communist-Socialist Romania, as guided by the Soviet Union's socialist example, had built many such resorts on the Black Sea and elsewhere in the Carpathian Mountains for the enjoyment and relaxation of the Romanian Communist Party workers, just like the NAZI-Socialists built their resorts for the NAZI workers-party members.

Interesting! NAZI Germany smelled like Socialism to me. As in Socialist Romania, the NAZIs were providing for their party members in a socialist way.

In the *How Socialist Was Adolf Hitler?* Alan Brown wrote that:

> The NAZI-Socialist party facilitated millions of state-subsidized holidays for all social classes who had to mix together on the excursions, cruises and hundreds of activities. Richard Grunberger noted that cabin allocation on the cruise ships was decided by the drawing of lots and not social status. [8]

I decided to investigate what else Hitler's NAZI-Socialist Germany did for the German people and found out that they did everything that the Communist-Socialist governments did for their proletariat. An even bigger eye-opener is that Hitler did some of these socialist things before the Communist-Socialist countries implemented them. Were the NAZI-Socialists the original socialists? Maybe not. These programs and activities were first implemented by Mussolini's Fascist (Socialist) party and called *Dopo lavoro* (after work). The program instituted by the Italian Fascist party reflected its underlying socialist principles.

As I dug deeper, I found *Kraft durch Freude* (Strength through Joy) and Schonheit *der Arbeit* (Beauty of Work) programs to inspire the German workers to enjoy life and work even harder. In Germany, NAZI-Socialism spared no expense in providing for the enjoyment of the people. Besides the resort, Colossus of Prora at Ruegen, they built a cruise ship, the *Wilhelm Gustloff*, a 25,000-ton ship for leisure and cruises on the Baltic Sea. I don't think Communist-Socialist Romania ever equaled these achievements on the Black Sea. But the Germans didn't stop there. Hitler ordered a people's car, the Volkswagen, for the everyday German to own, just like in America. The equivalent of the Volkswagen in the German Democratic Republic, East Germany, was the Trabant. After all, socialism continued under the Marxism-Socialism banner in East Germany.

Socialism promises heaven on earth, and if it can, it will deliver on those promises "as long as other people's money doesn't run out," as Margaret Thatcher allegedly said. Rewarding the population with entertainment and inexpensive vacations is a good morale booster after hard work. The other advantage of rewarding the people is the continuing indoctrination in the socialist cause—while you have them captive in a resort, on a cruise line, or in performances in theaters and movies. These and many more examples will convince you that:

Hitler was a first class Socialist.

Chapter 6. Who Was Adolf Hitler?

Adolf Hitler was a German-Austrian and a fanatic German nationalist, born in 1889 in Braunau am Inn in Austria, across the Inn River from Bavaria, Germany. He was the son of Alois and Klara Hitler, his father a customs official. Hitler's upbringing does not show anything special about him, and after his father's death, he dropped out of *Realschule*, secondary school. Having some talent in sketching and watercolor painting, he applied to the Academy of Fine Arts in Vienna and was declined entrance twice, although he was advised to try architecture, which he never pursued. Nonetheless, he considered himself an artist and an architect.

In spite of his lack of higher education, he was self-taught, reading books from the Library of the Association for Popular Education in Vienna, mostly in politics, history, and geography. He attended the opera many times, and his favorite composer was Richard Wagner. He was described as an aloof loner in his teen years, having very few friends. He also considered himself of the bourgeois class based on his father's profession. In Vienna, he worked odd jobs, but, considering himself an artist, he painted postcards of Vienna buildings and even sold them to a Jewish merchant.

He seethed with anger against anyone, Germans or foreigners who denigrated the German people. He hated the Hapsburg Monarchy of the Austrian-Hungarian Empire for treating all the empire's subjects equally, instead of elevating the German people and language above all the other *riffraff* nationalities. During the Vienna years, he developed his hatred of the Jews, who were tolerated by the empire and who prospered and increased their numbers in the city.

He moved to Munich, Bavaria, in Germany and volunteered in the German army to fight in World War I. He was a decorated soldier, receiving the Iron Cross Second Class and then the Iron Cross First Class, and his rank at the end of the war was corporal. After the war, he was an invalid, suffering from mustard gas wounds to his eyes. Germany's loss in the war seems to have been a great blow to his nationalistic feelings, and he believed the propaganda that Germany was stabbed in the back and was tricked into surrendering while still capable of winning. The culprits, besides the many German traitors, were the Jews, who got richer from the war.

Per the terms of the Armistice and the Treaty of Versailles after World War I, the German Army had to be reduced to only 100,000 soldiers, and Hitler was, consequently, discharged from the military. When he was still in the Army his job was to spy on radical groups. One of them being the DAP, the German Worker's party, a little-known nationalist movement. While attending his first meeting, he spoke up, and supposedly he discovered that he had oratory skills. The party chairman, Anton Drexler, insisted that he join in. According to Hitler, he was tormented over joining this party or any party at all, but he did realize that there was some affinity between his nationalistic beliefs and this party's agenda.

This party, or more accurately, movement, was so *large* that he was member number seven when he was admitted.

Other sources say that his number was 555, which might have been his number in the national movement rather than in the local Munich section. Soon after he joined, the movement changed its name to National Socialist German Workers Party, NSDAP.

Once a member, and because of his oratory skills, he assumed the position of propaganda officer, and to everyone's surprise, the people started to come to hear him and to join the party. At first, these meetings were held in Bier Halls, and eventually, as the number of listeners increased into the thousands, the meetings and rallies were moved to larger and larger venues. His oratory skills increased the membership in the National Socialist German Workers Party, and it became obvious that they had grown into a *real* party. NAZI was their nickname, although Hitler never referred to it as such, only National Socialist Party. He wrote the bylaws and created the final design of the swastika for the National-Socialist party and its flag.

The new nationalist party grew and became a dominant factor in the political arena of Bavaria. But either because Hitler was frustrated by the slow advance of their cause or because he was emboldened by Mussolini's coup d'état in Italy, he and others decided on a coup d'état against the Bavarian government. This was the *Putsch* of November 9, 1923, which failed miserably with several members shot dead. He and his surviving co-conspirators ended up in prison.

Although the *Putsch* of November 9, 1923, failed, it didn't discourage Hitler and the NAZI-Socialist Party from continuing. Hitler took the time to write his book *Mein Kampf* (*My Struggle*) during his stay in prison. He wrote about his coming of age and how his beliefs were formed. He outlined his National-Socialist philosophy and his tactics for taking power in Germany. He was released from prison in 1924, early, without serving his full sentence, but with the condition that he wouldn't be attempting another overthrow of the government. He was banned from public speaking until 1927.

It seems that he had learned his lesson and did not try another *Putsch*. He would take over the government through politics. Transitioning from rabble-rouser to respectable politician, he led the NSDAP to the first election in the Reichstag in 1928, gaining twelve seats. In 1929, the depression hit, and Germany plunged into despair and unemployment. Taking advantage of the financial crisis, Hitler and his rhetoric increased the party membership to 107 seats in the 1930 Reichstag election. Hitler ran for president of Germany against incumbent Paul von Hindenburg, but lost. The popularity of the NAZI-Socialist party increased, and in the 1933 election, it won 230 seats, the largest bloc in the Reichstag. Hitler wanted the chancellor's job but didn't get it. New elections were called again in 1933, and his party won 288 seats, 43.9% of the vote.

Although the NAZI party never achieved a majority in the Reichstag, it was the largest bloc, and by allying itself with other right-wing and nationalist parties and through political maneuvers, Hitler became the chancellor of Germany. Because of a communist, Marinus van der Lubbe, who allegedly set fire of the Reichstag building, he managed to obtain dictatorial powers by a majority vote in the Reichstag, after which he dissolved it. In 1934, he initiated the "Night of the Long Knives" in order to consolidate his power and gain the support of the military. He purged (executed) the entire leadership of the SA, the stormtroopers (Brownshirts - *Sturmtruppen*), including their leader Ernst Rohm, along with political enemies like Gregor Strasser —second in the NAZI-Socialist command—, Kurt von Schleicher —previous Chancellor—, and many others.

After the death of Paul von Hindenburg in 1934, the office of the president was abolished, and Adolf Hitler, the Chancellor of Germany, became a full dictator. He had already outlawed the German Communist Party along with other Marxist-Socialist parties in 1933, and after 1934, all political parties were outlawed except the National Socialist German Worker's Party, thereby changing Germany into a NAZI-Socialist totalitarian state.

By rearming Germany and undertaking socialist construction initiatives, Hitler resolved the depression-era financial crisis, creating jobs for the six million unemployed and starting a miracle recovery unparalleled in Europe. He received the congratulations of all major countries, including President Roosevelt of the United States, for solving the economic problems in Germany, and he became the envy of the rest of the world. Life improved for most Germans, and for the first time since the end of the Great War, Germans felt proud of their country and happy to put behind them the war and the Weimar democracy. In 1938, Hitler was named the "Man of the Year" by *Time Magazine*.

In 1938, Hitler announced the Anschluss, the unification of his native land Austria with Germany. After annexing Sudetenland from Czechoslovakia in 1938, in the spring of

1939, he occupied the rest of that country causing anxiety among the major powers in Europe. The years of economic build-up and rearmament caused scarcities in Germany. Although Hitler ordered armament production cuts and increased the manufacture of products for exports to grow Germany's foreign exchange holdings and be able to import raw materials for rearmament, the NAZI-Socialist government had reached the limits of its achievements and had to acquire new wealth, as all socialist countries eventually do. That new wealth, as he spelled it out in *Mein Kampf*, was to be found in new territories in the east, the USSR.

On September 1, 1939, National-Socialist Germany invaded Poland, conquering half of that country as previously decided under the Molotov-Ribbentrop agreement, leaving the other half for Stalin's Soviet Union to occupy. On September 3, 1939, Britain and France declared war on Germany for invading Poland, and World War II began. The NAZI-Socialist Wehrmacht occupied Norway, Denmark, and then Belgium, Netherlands, and Luxembourg. By 1940, they had conquered France, giving Hitler his early glory in the war.

His intent was always to invade and conquer the Soviet Union, to give Germans room to grow, *Lebensraum*. He even wrote of his intentions in *Mein Kampf*, but very few understood how serious he was. In 1941, he invaded the Soviet Union, and his army advanced to near St. Petersburg and Moscow and conquered Stalingrad.

In 1942, year after Japan attacked the United States and the US entered the war, Hitler's advancing armies were stopped. The United States provided the USSR with armament and technology to fight the Germans and helped Great Britain to continue the war. The US army landed in North Africa and, with Great Britain, defeated Rommel, after which the Allies landed in Sicily, continuing to defeat Fascist Italy and the German forces fighting there. The Soviet Union advanced on the East Front, and the Allies landed in Normandy in 1944, beginning the attack in the West.

Hitler was a racist and wanted a pure Aryan race in Germany. He and his government embarked on exterminating Jews, Gypsies, political enemies, and the feeble and deformed. The executions and extermination camps killed eleven million innocent people, just because they were the wrong race, or had the wrong politics or capabilities.

For me, as a grandfather of an autistic grandson, I am very angry to think that his life could be in danger under such a regime.

Attacked from the west and the east, Germany had lost the war by the spring of 1945. Trapped in his bunker in Berlin, shortly after marrying Eva Braun, Hitler and Eva committed suicide on April 30, 1945. The Soviet army was already in Berlin, and the war ended on May 8, 1945.

According to Joachim Fest, there has never been another man like Adolf Hitler:

> For he was, it has been said, the Rousseau, the
> Mirabeau, the Robespierre and the Napoleon of
> his revolution; he was its Marx, its Lenin, its
> Trotsky and its Stalin. . .. He nevertheless
> managed to achieve what all of them could not:

> he dominated his revolution in every phase,
> even in the moment of defeat. [2: pg 4]

Unfortunately, Adolf Hitler was not a Messiah, but Satan himself. Hitler came to power using his evil oratorical genius and political shrewdness, taking advantage of the desperate political and economic situation in Germany after the Great War, establishing a political party that incorporated nationalism and socialism, winning the hearts of millions of Germans, and being democratically voted into power in the hope that he would restore Germany to its great status. World War II was inevitable as you'll soon see.

Chapter 7. Why Did Hitler Choose Socialism?

Hitler understood well the nature of the human psyche and how to spellbind the German people into following him. And that could only be accomplished through a socialist movement, as he said in *Mein Kampf*:

> The Pan-German movement was right in its theoretical view about the aim of a German renascence, but unfortunate of its choice of methods. It was nationalistic, but unhappily not *socialistic* enough to win the masses. [5: pg 122] Emphasis added.

Socialism combined with nationalism was a formidable solution to gain power at that time in Germany, and he knew how to put it to use.

When he was young, Adolf Hitler never dreamed of becoming what he would become. He was not a noble (von), and for that reason alone he could not have become an officer in the military (Reichswehr). He was not wealthy, either from land or businesses. He didn't have any skills to earn him a decent living, nor did he have enough talent to become a great artist as he had hoped. He didn't have credentials for anything. He did not even know that he had oratory talents until he joined the DAP movement. With that talent, he could have a future in politics. However, he despised Marxist-Socialism as a Jewish fabrication. He could have joined other established nationalistic parties, but he would have had to start at the bottom. To reach the top would have taken him a long time. President Hindenburg always referred to him as *that Austrian corporal*, limiting his political aspirations and blocking him from becoming the German chancellor for years. Only by hook and by crook he managed to get the chancellorship and overcome Hindenburg's reluctance to get that position.

To obtain political power, one would have had to be of the nobility, an industrialist with money and connections, or an established politician. Hitler had tried force and failed. The democratic electoral process, however, might disguise the true National-Socialist revolution. As a political party, in a democratic country, it needed the support of a lot of people to achieve power. The voters would be happy for a while with nationalistic speeches, but nationalism would not feed the masses or improve their lives. Jobs and bread would, and this is how socialism entered into the equation of the new party-to-be.

As Hitler said:

> Thus, the reservoir from which the young movement must gather its supporters will primarily be the masses of our workers. [5: pg 340]

Hitler fully understood how the power of the masses/society/socialism would work to help his young party, NSDAP. He also was a true believer in socialism as a means to improve the life of all German nationals.

In Germany in the 1920s and 1930s, there were more than thirty parties, each one with a different agenda and doctrine. Out of all these parties the most prominent were:
(KPD) Kommunistische Partei Deutschlands—Communist German Party.
(SPD) Sozialdemokratische Partei Deutschlands—Socialist German Party.

Hitler Was a Socialists

(BVP) Bayerische Volkspartei—Bavarian People's Party
(DDP) Deutsche Demokratische Partei—German Democratic Party.
(DVP) Deutsche Volkspartei—German People's Party.
(DNVP) Deutschnationale Volkspartei—German National People's Party.
(Centre) Zentrumspartei —The Center Party
(NSDAP or **NAZI)** Nationalsozialistische Deutsche Arbeiterpartei—National Socialist German Workers' Party
Source: Wikipedia

There are certain threads that cross any society when it comes to politics:

1. Marxism-Socialism appeals mostly to the proletariat, the industrial workers, offering them a better life by abolishing the profit and the capitalist exploiters.

2. Democrat-Socialism appeals to middle and lower classes with a strong bias against the wealthy and redistribution of the wealth through higher taxation of the rich and nationalization of some of the economy.

3. Democratic parties cater to the middle and upper classes of different persuasions by giving them a voice in the governing of the country.

4. Christian/Catholic democratic parties appeal to their religious followers.

5. Provincial allegiances, such as the Bavarian party, appeal to people in those provinces.

6. Nationalism appeals to all the citizens of a country: the poor and the rich, the proletariat and the peasants, the intelligentsia and the uneducated, the Catholics and Lutherans, to all classes. But nationalism has a problem: it has weak appeal during peaceful times.

However, an equal-opportunity socialist party, allowing all classes, under the banner of nationalism—and without excluding anyone as the Socialist and Communist Parties did—was a winning formula.

In *Hitler* Joachim C. Fest described the ideology of National Socialism:

> Even more socialistic was the group's economic program: large landholdings were to be abolished, and all peasants were to be organized into agricultural cooperatives; small businesses were to be grouped in guilds; corporations with more than twenty employees were to be partially socialized. The group also advocated simplification of legislation and creation of a school system open to all classes. [2: pg 234]

If you don't know anything about socialism (not communism), read the above again, because socialism is well and concisely spelled out. And these *were* the beliefs that Hitler professed.

Hitler played both sides of the political spectrum. Being a nationalist, he was of the Right, and the industrialists loved him. Being a socialist, he was of the Left, but not of the Marxist-Socialist Left, although to many, he *sounded* like a regular leftist as the following attests:

> The nameless Bavarian plain-clothes [police]man who attended a demonstration of the NSDAP in the summer of 1921, and reported to his office that Hitler was 'nothing but . . . the leader of a second Red Army' had grasped the essence of the man more keenly than the conservative notables of 1933. [2: pg 368]

By his words, Hitler had convinced some observers that he was *the leader of a second Red Army*, a Bolshevik. However, unbeknownst to the conservatives (nationalists), he used them to advance NAZI-Socialism to establish himself as the Chancellor of Germany in 1933, and soon after as a dictator, while all along he was a socialist not only in name but in actions.

Although a socialist, he despised Marxist-Socialism, saying:

> It was only the Jew who succeeded, through falsifying the social idea and turning it into Marxism. [4]

This was the belief that Hitler held regarding the right formula for his party, not to be confused with Marxism, which had falsified the socialist ideals. By combining nationalism and socialism, the National-Socialist party, NSDAP, theoretically was able to appeal to everyone. Nationalism on an empty stomach can take you only so far. Promises for a better life appeal to everyone. Nationalism was the platform of the German National People's Party (DNVP) and didn't have much impact on voters. Marxism-Socialism, on the other hand, is an internationalist movement by decree and, therefore, anti-nationalist, another reason Hitler hated it.

Note: *Today, Internationalism has been replaced by Globalism.*

In five years, the NAZI-Socialists rose from 810 thousand votes to more than 17 million votes, from twelve seats in Reichstag in 1928 to 288 seats in 1933. Hitler's strategy worked, especially in the economic (depression) conditions of those times. The NAZI-Socialist party had the largest bloc of votes, followed by the SPD, the Socialist German Party, which controlled only 120 seats. As it grew, the NAZI-Socialist party had gained at every other parties' expense, except for the Communist and Center Parties.

But, really, how socialistic was Hitler? As socialistic as any socialist in the Marxist-Socialist parties.

Here is with Hitler said in his own words:

'National' and 'Social' are two identical conceptions. And similarly to be 'social' means so to build up the state and the community of the people that every individual acts in the interest of the community of the people and must be to such an extent convinced of goodness, of the honorable straightforwardness of this community of the people as to be ready to die for it.

Capitalism as a whole will now be destroyed, the whole people will now be free. We are not fighting Jewish or Christian capitalism; we are fighting every capitalism: we are making the people completely free. [4: Munich Speech April 12, 1922]

To him Nationalism and Socialism are one and the same. One cannot think of his nation and not think about the entire society, and he considered himself a true Socialist. Do not be fooled by the fanatical oratory of the Marxist-Socialists, claiming that they fight for the non-privileged. That propaganda applies to young people and to those socialist comrades of less than average intelligence. The higher a member rises in the party, the more pragmatic and fake he or she becomes. No idealistic socialist would allow the people to die of starvation or shoot them when they revolt, but Mao, Stalin, and Ceausescu all did exactly that in the name of socialism.

Who do the Democrat-Socialists claim to represent in the United States? The working people, the economically disadvantaged, the racial minorities. Have they kept their promises? Of course not. It is only propaganda and the expediency of acquiring political power.

If Hitler were such a big socialist, why didn't he join Marxism-Socialism or even the communist movement? The following is one of his reasons:

64

> The Jew's second instrument was the Marxist
> theory in and for itself. For directly one went
> on to assert that property as such is theft,
> directly one deserted the obvious formula that
> only the natural wealth of a country can and
> should be common property, but that that man
> creates or gains through his honest labor is his
> own, immediately the economic intelligentsia
> with its nationalistic outlook could, here too no
> longer co-operate: for this intelligentsia was
> bound to say to itself that this theory meant the
> collapse of any human [endeavor]. [4: Munich
> Speech July 28, 1922]

Pure Marxism stipulates that no man should exploit
another man and profit from it. Therefore, all private
property is confiscated by the state for the benefit of all.
The Marxists, Communists, and Socialists were invested
in that idea, which was appealing to the workers who
didn't own anything. But there were a lot of other people
who owned stuff, not necessarily big wealth, but enough
to give them pause about following the Marxist cause.
There were also the landless peasants who, although they
did not own land, desired more than anything else their
own plot of land; but under Marxism, that was wealth and
not theirs to obtain or keep.

To Hitler and all other socialists, Marxists included,
socialism is just a tool to acquire power. The people are
needed to fight for or elect a leader to power. Once in
power, if not kept in check, the entrapments of power will
make any human a despot. If a leader does not take
advantage of unchecked power, that leader's days are
numbered, and other wannabe despots waiting in the wings
will act. That's why all socialists belong in the same
infernal cauldron. They can rule only as dictators.

Hitler wanted to differentiate between his National-Socialist agenda and that of the Marxist-Bolsheviks, by saying:

> Bolshevism turns flourishing countrysides into a sinister waste of ruins; National Socialism transforms a Reich of destruction and misery into a healthy State and a flourishing economic life. Russia planned a world revolution and German workmen would be used but as cannon-fodder for bolshevism imperialism. [4: Nuremberg Speech September 14, 1936]

He only needed to point at the Soviet Union, during those times, to see what Marxism and its obsession with not allowing private property does to a country. Many people accepted the *better* socialist system of NAZI-Socialism in Germany and voted him into power.

From *The Program of the Party of Hitler* it is said:

> Only so will each one attain to the genuine Socialism, the communal feeling, the true life, win consciousness of security, and realize that only under the domination of this idea can an organic, national government arise from the present day system of robbery, and be of profit to the community, and to each member of the community. [6: pg 34]

Although averse to Marxism and confiscation of wealth, Hitler wanted all people to enrich themselves along with the community. The above statement sounds beyond socialism, more like communism.

Socialism is the best political system that will get you total political power.

Chapter 8. The Jews

The question is, why were the Jews so hated in Europe? Hitler did not invent anti-Semitism; it existed for centuries and still exists today. Not all countries in Europe hated the Jews equally. Surprisingly, anti-Semitism was rather mild in Germany compared to other European nations. Hundreds of thousands of Jews fought in the Great War for the Kaiser in the German army. But all that changed with Hitler's rise to power. To understand this irrational hatred, we have to go back in history to find out what happened.

The Roman Empire squelched the Jewish rebellion in the second century AD and demolished the temple in Jerusalem, enslaved the Jews, destroyed their towns, and chased them away from Judea, which was renamed Syria Palaestina and later Palestine, until the formation of the state of Israel. The Jews spread out through the Roman Empire as the Jewish Diaspora while adhering to their Judean religion. The Jews did not encounter any religious discrimination in the Roman Empire until Christianity replaced the multi-deity religions in the Empire. Since then, they migrated throughout Europe, settling in different places until they were persecuted and pushed out to relocate someplace else, where they were welcomed at first, then tolerated, and eventually chased out.

Under Christian-dominated Europe, the Jews were accused of killing Jesus Christ, although Roman Prefect Pontius Pilate crucified him, not for religious reasons but for messing with the money exchangers at the temple. The

Romans took seriously the loss of tax revenues that Jesus might have caused. Nevertheless, the stigma stuck, and considering that the Jews follow their own religion, the persecution was easily accepted by the Christian population of every country. As a persecuted minority, the Jews did not have enough time to settle in any one area and acquire land, the most common source of wealth until the Industrial Revolution.

The Jews turned to commerce and to moneylending to earn a living, which was disallowed by the church. Monetary capital became the specialty of many Jews to conduct their commerce and to lend to princes, kings, nobility, and others who could provide collateral to secure the loans. From before the Roman times, money in the form of gold or silver was used and therefore it was an asset that could be used to prosper.

In the past, many oppressed populations had been crushed by persecution. They gave up their distinctness and assimilated with the local populations. But not the Jews. They didn't abandon their culture and their religion, and aided by their religion, they toughened and succeeded. The Jews made the best of what they had, and they prospered, especially after the start of the Industrial Revolution when monetary capital was necessary to build machinery and factories. The Jews were not the only financiers or bankers in the world, but they had an early start. Generation after generation, they developed keen understanding of what wealth is and how it can be acquired. As bankers, they were the first ones to see new industries evolving and to see which ones prospered, how they prospered, and why they prospered. With that knowledge, it didn't take a great leap of faith for them to become industrialists themselves and to prosper even more.

Maintaining wealth cannot be done in ignorance. Good education was necessary. With wealth, Jewish parents were able to provide higher education for their children. Education became the path to a better life, and the Jews were disciplined and dedicated to making sure their children acquired knowledge and education. Of course, not every Jew could become a banker or an industrialist. Becoming a merchant was another way of prospering. Jews who did not like finances, enterprising, goldsmithing, or retail work but liked knowledge and education became professors, doctors, lawyers, journalists, accountants, or classical musicians.

These later trades, while not always generating great wealth, provided a comfortable living. (There was an anecdote about Israel after an influx of Soviet Jews: *There's a string quartet at every corner*.) And with Mediterranean weather, there were not enough jobs for all the freshly arrived weatherman to be employed, not to mention all the newsmen, lawyers, professors, and other white-collar workers from the USSR. Most of the Jewish immigrants didn't have skills in manufacturing, construction, agriculture, transportation, and the many other menial jobs a country needs. But they adapted, and some even worked on kibbutzim.

Did the European populations hate the Jews universally? For starters, anyone who is better off than you, has more than you, and so on is an object of envy. They don't have to be Jews, but since many of the well-to-do *were* Jews, the hatred was amplified. That many merchants were Jews made one wonder. That many doctors and lawyers were Jews raised suspicion. That many bankers, financiers, and stock-market investors were Jews was a sure sign of a cabal. Why were so many Jews professors, journalists, classical musicians, or political activists/instigators? They invented Marxism-Socialism and became leaders of leftist parties. Trotsky and Lenin were Jews, just as the German communist leaders Leo Jogiches, Paul Levi, and Rosa Luxemburg.

Acceptance to universities was difficult with so many young Jews vying for spots in law, medicine, economics, and other prosperous professions. On the other hand, you don't see many Jewish shoemakers, mechanics, agricultural workers, or assembly-line workers, only goldsmiths and diamond cutters. What's going on?

Many people thought—and many people still think—that there is a Jewish conspiracy. They are not Christians. They are clannish. They have connections to inside information to make them rich. Their professors are influencing our population's young minds. They are manipulating our opinions with their journalism and even influencing our politicians to play to their tune. They even instigated revolutions and wars to enrich themselves. After all, didn't Baron Rothschild, a Jew, say, "The time to buy is when there's blood in the streets"?

The evidence is plain as day, many may say. They have, we don't, and hatred followed.

Or perhaps they are smarter, although the Jews are the first to deny that. I counted 167 Jewish Nobel Laureates. I am Romanian-American, and I checked out how many Romanians of a country of twenty million achieved that success. Disappointingly, only four. The worldwide Jewish population is less than fifteen million.

Possibly, they work harder, more focused and more disciplined to achieve their goals for a more prosperous life. Maybe they're clear minded and stand up from the trenches where everyone is digging, stuck with our noses in the dirt, and they see a landscape different from what the rest of us see. And if that's the case, shouldn't we emulate them and do as they do?

Hating is easy. Emulating is hard. Therefore, people collectively hate the Jews because they are not like most of us. In Europe, the Jews were viewed as foreigners in spite of the fact that they spoke the language of the country they lived in. In many cases, unless they were Orthodox Jews, they were indistinguishable from the general population, not to mention that many gentiles have Jewish blood and that gentile blood is part of the Jewish blood. Otherwise, how would you have blue-eyed Jews? In the end, the races were intermixed, and the difference between Jews and gentiles is religion and culture, although Jewish religion is the foundation of Christianity and the culture is indistinguishable from that of the gentile culture.

Along came Hitler and NAZI-Socialism. All he had to do was fan the flames of smoldering hatred, the culmination of which was the killing of almost six million Jews.

I read about an article from a Spanish newspaper that said, and I paraphrase, Hitler's Germany eliminated a smart, educated, professional, wealthy section of the population. Seventy years later, Angela Merkel brought into Germany millions of uneducated, backwards non-Christians of a different culture from the Middle East.

These are the paradoxes of socialism, I may add.

Hitler considered capitalism, the stock exchange, democracy, and Marxism as the work of the Jews, where people were set to be antagonistic against each other for selfish reasons instead of doing what was best for the nation and people. Never mind that National-Socialism was antagonistic toward other races.

In many of his speeches, Hitler said:

> And the right has further completely forgotten that democracy is fundamentally not German: it is Jewish.
>
> The master stroke of the Jew was to claim the leadership of the fourth estate: he founded the Movement both of the Social Democrats and the Communists. His policy was twofold: he had his 'apostles' in both political camps.
>
> The Jews succeeded in isolating this new movement of the workers from all the nationalist elements. . . . More and more so to influence the masses that he persuaded those of the Right that the faults of the Left were the faults of the German workman, and similarly he made it appear to those of the left that the faults of the Right were simply the faults of the so-called 'Bourgeois,' and neither side noticed that on both sides the faults were the result of a scheme planned by alien devilish agitators . . . that Stock Exchange Jews should become the leaders of a Workers Movement.
>
> And one can see constantly how wonderfully the Stock Exchange Jew and the leader of the workers, how the Stock Exchange organ and the journal of the workers co-operate. They

both pursue one common policy and a single
aim. Mosses Kohn on the one side encourages
his association to refuse the worker's demands,
while his brother Isaac in the factory incites the
masses and shouts, "Look at them! They only
want to oppress you! Shake off your fetters." [4:
Munich Speech July 28, 1922]

Hitler addresses all the evils perceived by the Germans
and why their life was so bleak. The sentiments expressed
above were not new, as all the anti-Semites professed
them, but Hitler took them to a new height, proclaiming
that the Jews control the workers and the bourgeoisie for
their selfish gains and to the detriment of everyone.
Unfortunately, this polemic fell on receptive ears of
religious hatred and economic envy against the Jews, and
Hitler gained in popularity. With the rise of National-
Socialism, a perfect storm was brewing, and it culminated
with the Holocaust.

One statement from *How Socialist Was Adolf Hitler?* by
Alan Brown shows what the understanding of genocide
and socialism was in the 1930s:

It is notable that no German socialist in the
1930s or earlier ever sought to deny Hitler's
right to call himself a socialist on grounds of
racial policy. In the age when the socialist
tradition of genocide was familiar, that would
have sounded merely absurd. . . .. From Engels'
article in 1849 down to the death of Hitler,
everyone who advocated genocide called
himself a socialist, and no exception has been
found. [8]

These sentiments during those times are
shocking by today's morals, but along with

eugenics, they were widely accepted by the society and the socialists back then.

Chapter 9. Pave the Way to Seize Political Power

Germany was in bad shape after losing the First World War: They were hurting economically and militarily, their national prestige was in ruins, and after the war, in 1918, there was a revolution that lasted a year and threatened to convert Bavaria into a Marxist-Socialist state. It didn't happen, and instead Germany became a republic, the Weimar Republic, with a parliament, chancellor, and president. Things could have turned out better, but they didn't. The time became ripe for a new revolution, as Germany continued in turmoil and most Germans felt betrayed by the Treaty of Versailles.

Eventually Hitler came along and offered a new direction and began to take the following steps to seize political power:

9.1. Ideology—Define Hate and Offer Hope

The ideology of the NAZI-Socialist party was German, ethnic nationalism, pan-Germanism, anti-democracy, anti-capitalism, anti-communism and anti-Marxist-socialism, anti-Semitism, anti-social conservatism, reform of the German Reich into an authoritarian rule, and a classless society.

According to Joachim C. Fest:

> Anton Drexler had grasped the spirit of the age.
> For the DAP defined itself as a classless
> "socialist organization led only by German

leaders." Drexler's "inspired idea" was to reconcile nationalism and socialism." [2: pg 117]

Anton Drexler was the leader of the DAP (German Workers Party) in Bavaria, and he inspired the directives of the early movement to be a socialist party but not of a Marxist-Socialist variety, which was international in nature, and not controlled by non-Germans, as was the case for the Socialist party and the Communist party in Germany, in particular, that were controlled by Moscow.

Political movements start in a country with a disgruntled group—for economic, political, cultural, religious, ethnic, and many other reasons. Not all these movements become political parties, but the ones that enter politics need to have an agenda based on *hate* toward the culprits that are blocking the brighter future as the party sees it and *hope* to remedy the current faults and secure a better future. A movement based solely on one or the other will be unbalanced and confuse its followers—and it will unravel.

For the NAZI-Socialists the *hate* was toward the humiliation of the Treaty of Versailles, the punishing war reparations, the exclusion of Germany from any world affairs, and the Jews.

The political and economic ineptitude of the Weimar democratic government caused additional hate and disillusionment among people. The enemies of Germany and therefore of National-Socialism were enumerated clearly by Hitler.

Hitler said about democracy:

> Democracy is the canal through which bolshevism lets its poison flow into the separate countries and lets them work there long enough for these infections to lead to a crippling of

intelligence and of the force of resistance. [4: Nuremberg Speech September 14, 1936]

About capitalism, the stock exchange, international monetary institutions, and Jews, to which Germany was subjugated, Hitler said:

> Christian capitalism is already as good as destroyed, the international Jewish Stock Exchange capital gains in proportion as the other loses ground. It is only the international Stock Exchange and loan capital, the so-called "supra-state capital" which receives its character from the single supra-state nation which is itself national to the core, which fancies itself to be above all other nations, which places itself above other nations and which already rules over them. [4: Munich Speech April 12, 1922]

About hate for capitalism and Marxism and giving hope for the general welfare of the people, Hitler said:

> Capitalism and Marxism are one and the same. They grow on the same intellectual stem. There is a whole world of difference between them and us, their bitterest opponents. Our whole conception of the construction of society differs widely from theirs. It is neither a class-struggle nor class-selfishness, but our chief law is the general welfare. [6: pg 65]

Hitler attacks the stock exchange:

> One thing raises itself above them all: the World Stock Exchange which has become the master of the people.
>
> Capital is not the master of the State, but its servant. [4: Speech April 13, 1923]

The words above sound awfully familiar, just like socialist Bernie Sanders, who said:

> The reality is that fraud is the business model
> of Wall Street. . ... In fact the greed of Wall
> Street and corporate America is destroying the
> very fabric of our nation . . . and that is if Wall
> Street does not end its greed, we will end it for
> them.

As Bernie Sanders wishes, his Democrat-Socialist State would interfere with private enterprises and the source of capital from which all other wealth is derived. Bernie Sanders and Adolf Hitler agree.

How about what another socialist, Elizabeth Warren, said:

> Take on Wall Street so that the big banks can
> never again threaten the security of our
> economy.

Elizabeth Warren and Adolf Hitler agree that no other entity but the state can assure us of a secure economic and financial system. Who knew! I wonder if Elizabeth Warren ever heard that her concept of the Communist-Socialist world collapsed disastrously?

Adolf Hitler, Bernie Sanders, Elizabeth Warren, and all other socialists are united against capitalism and the financial institutions. Money means power and *they* want total control over it.

The Left, all other Marxists and leftist parties, were a common enemy to Hitler, and he said:

> The left is forced more and more to turn to
> Bolshevism. . ... They realize quite accurately
> that the people is beaten so long as Brain and
> Hand can be kept apart . . . the Socialist is
> coined only by men who see in it a means for
> disintegrating a nation. [4: Speech April 12, 1922]

In the above speech, Hitler is warning that socialism is turning to the left, to Bolshevism, because the Brain

(Intellectuals) and Hand (Workers) are disunited. And considering what the Bolsheviks have done to Russia, he considers this movement the disintegration of the nation. As a socialist, not to be confused with Marxism-Socialism, he's warning that Marxism-Socialism will slide into Bolshevism/Communism.

During the early part of the twentieth century in Germany, the intelligentsia was nationalistic—unlike American universities today, which are Marxist—and Hitler appealed to this group to reject Marxism as a ruinous economic idea and join NAZI-Socialism, and said:

> But it will be a sorry day for them when this Socialist idea is grasped by a Movement which unites it with the highest National pride . . . and thus places the Nation's Brain, its intellectual workers, on this ground. [4: Speech April 12, 1922]

Hitler makes the point that when socialism and nationalism are united under the National-Socialist party, they could stop the advance of Bolshevism. He made great efforts to include the intellectuals in his movement, along with all strata of the population in addition to the factory workers.

After blasting the Left, Hitler turns to the Right, accusing them of not recognizing the danger of addressing the ills of the nation and the people and being more concerned with being elected and securing high political positions.

He said:

> There remains then the Right. And this party of the Right meant well, but it cannot do what it would because up to the present time it has failed to recognize a whole series of elementary principles. These gentlemen still persist in believing that it is a question of being elected

to a Landtag [Parliament] or of posts as ministers or secretaries. [4: Speech April 12, 1922]

Who can offer hope to Germany? National-Socialism.

This should be a valid warning of our political situation in our country, the United States. Congress has a low approval rating, and we're divided like never before between the Left and the Right. If this situation continues unabated and we fall into a deep economic depression or any type of anarchy, like a pandemic caused by China Wuhan Coronavirus, the time will be ripe for one party, totalitarian government to be elected to power. There is no National-Socialist movement in this country, but the neo-Marxism-Leninism is strong and about to take over America.

By the way, this scenario played out in Venezuela under Hugo Chavez in 1998. Venezuela was a democratic country at the end of twentieth century. Hugo Chavez, just like Hitler, attempted a revolution, failed, and was imprisoned. After his release from prison, his party became a populous party and won power through elections. Since then, it has been ever downward for Venezuelans.

About Marxism Hitler said:

> By Marxism I understand a doctrine which in principle rejects the idea of the worth of personality, which replaces individual energy by the masses and thereby works the destruction of our whole cultural life. . .. This movement is distinguished by incredible terror, which is based on a knowledge of mass

psychology. [4: Before the Munich Court Speech February 26, 1924]

Although he's got it right about how Marxism-Socialism views the individual, a worker bee with no mind of its own, his NAZI-Socialism was as horrible as Marxism-Socialism when it came to individual freedom and the role of the individual in Germany. He envisioned the German citizen molded by Nationalist-Socialism just as the USSR envisioned the *new Soviet citizen* molded by Marxism-Leninism.

Hitler plainly recognized that National-Socialism was a carbon copy of Marxism without the entanglements of a Democrat-Socialist system. He said:

> These new methods of political struggle do go back to the Marxists in their essentials. I needed only to take over these methods and develop them, and in essentials I had what we needed. I needed only to pursue consistently what the Social Democrats interrupted ten times over, because they wanted to carry out their revolution within the framework of a democracy. National Socialism is what Marxism could have been had it freed itself from the absurd, artificial link with a democratic system. [2: pg 126]

In this case, Hitler talks about the German Socialist Democrat party, which, unlike the communists, wanted to obtain the majority in the Reichstag through democracy and maintain a democratic state. Hitler recognizes that this was a grave mistake and should not be followed. True socialism cannot exist in a democracy, only in the totalitarian system that NAZI-Socialism aspired to become.

As for hope, Hitler promised to get out of the Versailles Treaty, to bring back prestige for Germany, to create a stable political system under one-party rule, and to provide prosperity for all. In general, the NAZI-Socialists will undue all the evils that oppressed Germany. Although the details were vague, people believed and followed him.

9.2. Propaganda

The best product or idea in the world will not sell without promotion, a.k.a. *propaganda*.

Nationalist feelings were widely embraced throughout Germany, and nationalist-style movements were many, but only good propaganda would coalesce the people's sentiments to follow one party and listen to one leader. From *Mein Kampf*:

> The receptivity of the great masses is very limited, and their intelligence is small, but their power of forgetting is enormous . . . all effective propaganda must be limited to a very few points and must harp on these in slogans until the last number of the public understands what you want him to understand by your slogan. [5: pg 180-181]

Hitler fully understood propaganda and how to influence the masses. The basic principles were the same before Hitler and remain the same since. All politicians understand and use these principles when they campaign. Nowadays the leftist media in the US harp on one point and one point only, until you understand their party's line.

Hitler said:

> We are National Socialist fanatics. . .. We know only one interest and that is the interest of our people. [4: Munich Speech May 1, 1923]

Propaganda must be delivered with the most eagerness and passion to instill in people the message. He was not joking about fanaticism. A few good fanatics are worth one hundred lame followers.

Hitler's job was to consolidate and add as many members as possible to the National-Socialist movement. Here it is in Hitler's words from *Mein Kampf*:

> Today, when the ballot of the masses decides, the chief weight lies with the most numerous groups, and this is the first: *the mob of the simple and credulous.*
>
> The art of propaganda lies in *understanding the emotional ideas of the great masses* and finding, through psychologically correct form, the way to the attention and thence to *the heart of the broad masses.* [5: pg 242, 180] Emphasis added.

Don't hold it against Hitler when he said "the mob of the simple and credulous." This was true during Hitler's time and during the time of the Roman Empire. It is true today and will be true forever. There is a lot of truth in P.T. Barnum's statement that, "There's sucker born every minute." I might say there's a sucker born every second nowadays, and they are easy and credulous prey for the politicians or dishonest media.

In case you were not aware, most mainstream media in the United States and abroad are socialist; therefore, the above statement from socialist Hitler tells how this media propaganda is conducted. Remember when Chuck Schumer cried while opposing President Trump's ban on travel from certain Muslim countries? Didn't those tears go to your heart, even if we were trying to keep the terrorists out? Do you remember, too, the fanatic and hysterical demonstrations against the ban at airports?

Remember when the media showed the illegal immigrants from south of the border sleeping on the floor in detention centers or kids taken away from their "parents"? How inhumane! you might have thought. But bringing kids along on a 2,000-mile trek to our southern border was not inhumane but heroic. And 30% of the "parents" were not even related to the kids. Everything said was intended to appeal to our sentiments—and ignore the truth.

"The art of propaganda lies in understanding the emotional ideas of the great masses," and they sold it to us, in a socialist, emotional style that Trump is a heartless human being. Obama did the same and more to the illegal immigrants, but he was a Marxist and was untouchable.

Here's what Hitler thought about how to get to the masses:

> Above all be popular, he argued; it must not be aimed toward the intelligentsia but always and exclusively to the masses, and its level must be adjusted to the most limited intelligence among those it is addressed to. [2]

Which of the following is more appealing to the masses?

Our goal is the emancipation of the disenfranchised and forgotten.

or

Redistribute the wealth from the rich to the poor.

If you feel that the proletariat is exploited, as Comrade De Blasio, Democrat-Socialist Mayor of New York, wants you to believe, which of the messages is easier to understand?

Be popular and speak in plain language. When candidates run for office, who gets most of the votes? The candidate that is popular and known or the candidate who is unknown? Were Hillary Clinton and Donald Trump popular? Yes. Who knew Ben Carson? Or Jim Gilmore or George Pataki outside Virginia and New York? Many people don't even know who the VP of the United States is, or they think Nancy Pelosi is a Republican if they see her picture.

Hitler unveiled some more points about propaganda:

> Furthermore, effective propaganda must concentrate on a few plausible points and hammer away at these in the form of slogans. It must always appeal to emotions, never to the intellect, and must eschew any attempt at objectivity. Not even the shadow of a doubt in the rightness of one's own cause is permissible; propaganda must present love or hate, right or wrong, truth or lie, never half this way or half that way. [2]

Use simple words that the masses recognize and instigate love or hatred in the listener. Do not be concerned, but believe in the lie you're telling, because after repeating it so many times the lies will become the truth. As Joseph Goebbels said: "Repeat a lie often enough and it becomes the truth."

These are tried and true principles of propaganda that Hitler mastered. With a passionate delivery, he fired up the masses to believe in National-Socialism. Pay attention to what current politicians are telling us and how they tell it to us. Every coin has two sides, but they only talk about their side of the coin as if theirs is the only one-sided coin.

In Communist-Socialist Romania, all workers had to attend political meetings once a week at their job location. No different than attending church on Sunday, except it was during working hours on weekdays. These meetings reinforced the Communist-Socialist party's propaganda. Nowadays, you may not realize that you participate in *daily socialist propaganda meetings.* When? where? Through the socialist mainstream media every time you turn on the TV. For days on end, you'll hear the same slogans from most channels. As shown by Hitler, *"All effective propaganda must be limited to a very few points and must harp on these in slogans until the last number of the public understands what you want him to understand by your slogan."*

During the first term of President Trump you heard the following slogans:

Russia, Russia, Russia, Russia, Russia, Russia, Russia, Russia,

Recession, Recession, Recession, Recession, Recession, Recession,

Obstruction of Justice, Obstruction of Justice, Obstruction of Justice,

Constitutional Crisis, Constitutional Crisis, Constitutional Crisis,

Impeachment, Impeachment, Impeachment, Impeachment, Impeachment,

Racist, Racist, Racist, Racist, Racist, Racist, Racist, Racist, Racist, Racist,

Blood on his hands, Blood on his hands, Blood on his hands

Need I say more? The more Media channels spew fake news, the more believable it is.

Hitler Was a Socialists

Hitler said:

> Nothing can prove that more clearly than the mere conception of class war, the slogan that the rule of the bourgeois must be replaced by the rule of the proletariat. That means that the whole question becomes one of a change in a class dictatorship, while our aim is the dictatorship of the people, i.e. the dictatorship of the whole people, the community. [4: Berlin, Congress of the German Work Front – Speech of May 10, 1933]

Hitler is contrasting the difference between the Communist dictatorship of the *proletariat* in the USSR with the National-Socialist dictatorship of the *whole* people, not only one class, the proletariat, replacing another class, the bourgeoisie, but all people, the community of people.

In the United States today, class war, interpreted as communist propaganda, may not be accepted by many people. That's why the class war was replaced by race war, something that the media has worked at long and hard to pound into our brains, making just about anyone, especially of the Left, believe that we live in a racist country, *systemic racism*. I have lived in the USA for almost fifty years, and as far as I am concerned, the racial situation has continually improved. I have never seen any racism at work. On the contrary, many qualified white people, including me, were bypassed by non-whites. Out of nowhere systematic racism appears, as instructed in schools.

In his speeches, Hitler said:

> It is self-evident that where this democracy rules, the people as such are not taken into consideration at all. The only thing that matters is the existence of a few hundred gigantic capitalists who own all the factories and their stock and, through them, control people. The masses of the people do not interest them in the least. They are interested in them just as were our bourgeois parties in former times—only when elections are being held, when they need the votes. Otherwise, life of the masses is a matter of complete indifference to them. [4: Berlin, Rheinmetall-Borsig Works – Speech of Decembern10, 1940]

This, too, sounds similar to what's happening in United States today with our politicians. Hitler drummed against the democracy and against how the capitalists are controlling democracy and that no politician cares about you until the elections.

Socialist Bernie Sanders pointed at the same problems with our democracy and the effect the wealthy have on democracy:

> As a result of the Citizens United Supreme Court decision, American democracy is being undermined by the ability of the Koch brothers and other billionaire families. These wealthy contributors can literally buy politicians and elections by spending hundreds of millions of dollars in support of the candidates of their choice. We need to overturn Citizens United and move toward public funding of elections so that all candidates can run for office without being beholden to the wealthy and powerful.

Hitler Was a Socialists

Elizabeth Warren had the following to say about the same subject Hitler once spoke about:

> The over-representation of Wall Street banks in senior government positions sends a bad message. It tells people that one—and only one—point of view will dominate economic policymaking.

Considering what Adolf Hitler, Bernie Sanders, and Elizabeth Warren said, Sanders and Warren are either "fascists" like Hitler—or Hitler was a socialist

Here are words of warning from Hitler's speeches against the opposition on the Left and Right:

> And thus the Left is forced more and more to turn to Bolshevism. . .. So long therefore as the Socialist idea is coined only by men who see in it a means for disintegrating a nation, so long they can rest in peace. . .. But it will be a sorry day for them when this Socialist idea is grasped by a Movement which unites it with the highest National pride, with Nationalist defiance.
> The party of the Right have lost all energy. . ..
> In the Left there is somewhat more energy, but it is used for the ruin of Germany." [4: Munich – Speech of April 12, 1922]

An interesting statement about Germany, resembling the same situation in the United States today: The Right-Republicans are asleep, while the Left-Democrats charge ahead with all the zeal and fanaticism of a religious belief.

In *The Program of the Party of Hitler: The National Socialist German Worker's Party*, it is said:

> The people in control are totally unable to stem the chaos. Crushed from above by taxation and

interest payment, menaced from below by the grumblings of the submerged workers, they have bound themselves blindly to a State controlled by capitalism, while the exploiters of the present chaos suffer them to remain in power merely as slave drivers over the laboring masses.

The sham State of today oppressing the working classes and protecting the pirated gains of bankers and Stock Exchange speculators, is the arena for reckless private enrichment and for the lowest political profiteering. . ... The power of money . . . holds absolute control, and exercises corrupting, destroying influence on State. [6: pg 31]

These socialist cries against the evil of capitalism are as good as it gets, coming from the mouth of Hitler and his associates. If you heard the above statement today, you'd assume it was coming from Bernie Sanders or Elizabeth Warren or other leftists, not from Hitler and his NAZI-Socialist party.

9.3. Establish the Political Party, Its Symbol, Flag and Newspaper

On January 5, 1919, Anton Drexler formed the Munich German Worker's Party—DAP—a nationalist and anti-Semitic organization similar to other like-minded movements throughout Germany and Austria. It was called a party, but it had no elected officials. The villains were the German traitors who caused the loss of the war and the Jews who were enriching themselves and destroying the German nation.

At the end of September 1919 Adolf Hitler joined the DAP and with Hitler's approval the party's name was changed to NSDAP, the National Socialist German Worker's Party, borrowing the name from a similar party in Austria. The NAZI-Socialism political movement grew to the point that it became a true political party. To emphasize the party's identity, Hitler needed to create symbols, such as a flag and emblem. The Communist German Party—KDP or Kommunistische Partei Deutschlands—had the red flag and the communist emblem of the hammer and sickle. The NAZI-Socialists had nothing other than a name. Considering himself an artist, Hitler undertook the task of designing these symbols. The swastika had been used by other German nationalist movements in the past, having been borrowed originally from the Hindu religion, where it is a symbol of good luck, and Hitler redesigned it per his personal taste. He chose red for the color of the flag, indicating the *socialist* affiliation. That made the communists *see* red!

The emblem, the swastika, was placed on a round white background on the red flag. The party members and the SA—storm troopers—wore arm bands with the NAZI flag and swastika to identify themselves as NAZIs.

Hitler borrowed the fascist salute of Mussolini's Fascist Party, which became associated later with *Heil Hitler*. NSDAP bought the newspaper *Völkischer Beobachter* that became the party's official newspaper, the instrument of NAZI-Socialist propaganda.

And so, the National-Socialist party was ready to take over Germany.

The NAZI Socialist Party flag and later the German flag.

There is something to be said about the swastika. It is an unsettling image. That is because the symbol itself is made out of a square. Unlike rectangles, squares are unsettling in the emotion they impart. The circle is a soft symbol, comforting. In Buddhism, the square represents the earthbound while the circle represents heaven, expressing the connection between human and divine. To me, the circle has not softened the square image, and it feels unsettling, perhaps the effect sought by Hitler all along.

Similarly, Lenin had a Communist symbol designed for his party, the hammer and sickle, the factory worker and the agricultural worker united in their struggle against oppression and exploitation. The symbol is rounded up by the sickle, making a soft image, but the sharp point of the sickle also makes it a threatening image. The two deadly symbols side by side below:

9.4. Infiltrate the Unions and Convert Them into Party Members

Any political movement needs supporters and members. Since the NAZI-Socialist party was a socialist party, the recruits would come most naturally from the working people. But the proletariat was already monopolized by the German Communist and Social-Democratic parties. The NAZI-Socialists were undeterred by these facts. The NAZI members, in order to maintain good status in the party, were responsible for recruiting three new members. Unlike the German Communist and Social-Democrat parties, which appealed mostly to the proletariat, the NAZI-Socialists appealed to a broader segment of the population, including peasants, intellectuals, merchants, white-collar workers, government employees, and law-enforcement officers. Even some members of the military and many industrialists joined in, the latter because they were less afraid of NAZI-Socialism than of the German Communist Party, which definitely was planning to kill them.

Recruiting a union worker meant one less member of the Communist or Socialist parties. Joseph Goebbels many times positioned his car at the exits of factories to sermonize and recruit workers to NAZI-Socialism. His car, with the engine running, was positioned for a quick escape in case the workers became violent.

Hitler did not consider establishing NAZI-Socialist unions. The unions were the domain of the Socialist and Communist parties, and they were guarded jealously. Obtaining additional political power did not justify the effort. Later, however, the NAZI-Socialists took over all the unions and threw the union leaders in jail.

Dumitru Sandru

9.5. Infiltrate the Police, Justice, Government Employees, and the Military

It pays to have friends in the police and the military in case you break the law and need protection. Since the police were not fans of the communists and had a nationalist predisposition, they were easy targets for NAZI-Socialist propaganda and responded eagerly to recruitment efforts.

Similarly, the justice departments were nationalistically inclined and many, if not members of the party, were sympathizers with the NAZI. In his *Putsch* trial, the judge was sympathetic to the NAZI cause and allowed Hitler to take over the trial and declare his pristine intentions of saving the country from the Marxist-Socialist menace. His sentence was far more lenient than what the crime he committed demanded. His foreign citizenship was not considered seriously, and he was not to be deported after serving his sentence. In prison, he received preferential treatment and was allowed an unlimited number of visitors and the power to continue leading the NAZI-Socialist movement from behind bars. That's where he wrote *Mein Kampf*, My Struggle. Rudolf Hess typed the manuscript from Hitler's dictations. Eight months later he was released early from prison.

In the United States police forces have not been infiltrated by the Marxists—yet. But that cannot be said of the FBI, which *has* been infiltrated by Marxists. FBI agents are required to have bachelor's degrees, preferably master's degrees, and the newly minted graduates will have been indoctrinated into the Neo-Marxism-Leninism cause. Remember Trump and Russia? Who planted all those lies and caused such consternation in our country for two years? The FBI and the US Justice Department. James Comey, Andrew McCabe, Lisa Page, Peter Strzok, and who knows how many more like them were involved in setting up an elected American president, Donald Trump, as an agent of Putin. The hoax investigation of Robert Mueller found nothing. The Gestapo-style arrest of Roger Stone should be an embarrassment for our law enforcement. It reminded me of the secret police arrests in Communist-Socialist countries—in the middle of the night, coming with overwhelming forces to arrest an old man in shorts and T-shirt while asleep. Who in the justice department ordered and approved such a *Communist-Socialist secret police* arrest? Or maybe that's the norm of the future, arrests à la Communist-Socialist style to instill fear in the population.

The government bureaucracy was another target for the NAZI-Socialist party, an essential one. When coming into power, the transition is easier if many government employees are members of your party. Hitler did better than that. Besides trying to recruit the bureaucrats, the NAZI-Socialist party set up a shadow government with departments mimicking what the official government departments were doing, sort of learning the ropes to be ready. When they took power, the NAZI bureaucrats assumed the essential positions in the government without being slowed down by the old deep state.

The military was not allowed to take political sides and had to stay neutral. But considering the fury with which Hitler attacked the World War I allies, promising to bring

Germany back to its old glory, many in the military became sympathizers and even secret members of the NAZI-Socialist Party.

In the USA today, the police departments are leaning conservative, perhaps because the new recruits did not go to universities to be indoctrinated into Marxism-Socialism. To solve that problem, there is a great effort today to restructure (re-image) the police departments, to change their character from law-enforcement agencies to social aid agencies. I hope the criminals will appreciate this and stop robbing, burglarizing, and murdering. As a note, if the USA were to become a socialist country, the police would become the *state police* to protect the state from its citizens. The old police will be missed, considering how brutal the socialist police will become. I speak from experience.

9.6. Infiltrate the Educational System

The most effective way to spread propaganda is by indoctrinating the young minds, employing teachers who share your political beliefs. Therefore, the drive was to convert as many teachers as possible to NAZI-Socialism, by requiring each party member to recruit from social and athletic clubs or from any organization or group of people that expanded the party's influence and its ability to influence young minds.

National-Socialism needed to infiltrate academia as well, which was not difficult. Those were different times in Germany. Socialist professors were fired and banned from obtaining employment in any German university —

unlike the United States today, where the conservative professors are fired or simply not employed. Karl Marx, as a leftist, could not get a professorial job and survived on handouts from Friedrich Engels, who was a Capitalist-Socialist. It was OK for him to exploit his workers, but not for the rest of the bourgeoisie.

Hitler said:

> They realize quite accurately that a people is beaten so long as Brain and Hand can be kept apart. [4]

In addition to brawn, Hitler needed brains to make his revolution a reality, and he expended great effort to court and recruit the intelligentsia. Unlike the USSR, where Stalin sent entire generations of intelligentsia to the gulag, Hitler nourished them—unless they were Marxists.

In the United States, the Marxist-Socialists have infiltrated and dominate our schools and universities today, indoctrinating all students in Marxism-Socialism beliefs and in hatred of free enterprise. Generations of these young people since the mid-sixties are now working in the media, Hollywood, corporate America, and the government. The socialists in the USA don't have to establish shadow governments and be ready to take over. The deep-state has been infiltrated and it is more and more dominated by Marxists-Socialists.

9.7. Infiltrate the Media

The newspaper is a very powerful propaganda machine. People's beliefs are shaped by what they read. In the 1930s, people relied mostly on the papers for their news.

The radio was relatively new but became more popular after Hitler was in power. The only other audio-visual propaganda was in the news clips in movie theaters.

In the Germany of those times, as in Europe today, the newspapers were published under the auspices of political parties. The National-Socialists had many newspapers as the news was mostly local, but the main publication of NAZI-Socialism was the *Völkischer Beobachter* (The National Observer) that facilitated spreading NAZI-Socialist propaganda. Infiltrating the other politically oriented newspapers' editorial and production departments or inserting loyalists within them was difficult. It was not until the NAZI-Socialists took power that other media outlets were shut down or controlled by them.

The radio was a rather new propaganda tool, and Goebbels was successful in using it. Megaphones blasted Hitler's speeches at every street corner.

In Communist-Socialist countries, all media is controlled by the party, and only the party's point of view is disseminated. Producing an independent newspaper—and especially an opposition newspaper—is a crime. Even typewriters were registered since they were viewed as tools of anti-socialist propaganda.

In the USA today, the media is completely under the influence of the new Marxists-Socialists, and the news they release is Left biased. I wonder who is the American Joseph Goebbels, manipulating the information released through all the channels of media. You don't think that's possible? Pay attention to the news on ABC, CBS, NBC, MSNBC, CNN, and others every day. It is as if all of them are reading from the same leftist script.

9.8. Establish Militant Agitator Groups to Voice Loudly the Party Line

Although Hitler was a great orator—mesmerizing his audiences with promises of a great Germany and jobs for everyone while blaming the Jews, the financiers, the bankers, the capitalists, and foreign powers—but he was only one man and one microphone. To expand the message, he needed many more good speakers to influence people into joining the NAZI-Socialist party. He opened propaganda schools to train good orators in public speaking to spread the NAZI-Socialist beliefs. This undertaking served him well when he was barred from public speaking for four years after his release from prison. His deputies carried on and kept his message alive, and the party gained new adherents.

With the start of the 1928 elections, Hitler performed as many public speeches as possible. He flew from city to city to promote National-Socialism. Later on, he used the radio to propagate his message, accessing many more people than at public gatherings.

My father, when he was a kid, remembers hearing Hitler on the radio all the away in Romania. There were many Swabian Germans in that part of the Romania. One of them had a radio and played it for the neighbors, interpreting to the Romanians what Hitler said.

The following are examples of what Hitler thought about indoctrinating and capturing the attention of the German people:

> "Anyone who interprets National Socialism merely as a political movement knows almost nothing about it," Hitler declared. "It is *more than a religion*: it is the determination to create a new man." [2: pg 533] Emphasis added.

More than a religion? In other words, fanaticism. All socialist, nationalist, or Marxist movements demand religious fanaticism among their members. As for "create a new man," this goal is identical to what Lenin and Stalin wanted to create: *The Soviet Man.*

Continuing, Hitler said:

> We as National Socialists and members of the German Workers Party . . . must be on principle the most fanatical Nationalists. [4: Munich – Speech of April 12, 1922]

No political movement that does not show total fanaticism, with a religious zeal, can achieve its ultimate goals. Lukewarm speeches with no conviction are not a winning proposition. Most certainly, Hitler took notice of how fanatical the Marxist-Socialists were in promoting their cause.

In one of his speeches he said:

> Power in the last resort is possible only where there is strength, and that strength lies not in the dead weight of numbers but solely in energy. Even the smallest minority can achieve a mighty result if it is inspired by the most fiery, the most passionate will to act. [4: Munich – Speech of April 12, 1922]

Quality of followers is more important than quantity of followers. The dedication, the blind belief that the National-Socialist party cause was the answer for Germany. The belief in one's party had to be more than religious, just as today's socialists believe to a point that religious beliefs are replaced by the party's beliefs.

When President Trump began building the wall at the southern border and denying asylum to the illegal immigrants, a small but very vociferous group of people began protesting at the border against that policy. They made the five o'clock news, and that was their intention. The majority of the population stood by passively wondering who was right or wrong, while tens of thousands of illegal immigrants were coming in caravans to the United States borders.

Anything that is accomplished anywhere is started and pushed through by a minority of fanatical people. Lenin did not have the majority even within the Bolshevik party. Most of the Bolsheviks wanted to align themselves with the Mensheviks and other socialist parties to take power through democracy. Lenin, just like Hitler, disagreed, and he acted in St. Petersburg by taking over the parliament and soon after invaded the Winter Palace and took the Tsar and his family hostage. In the aftermath, the October revolution began.

9.9. Subdue and Intimidate the Opposition

Opposition is the enemy of a party and it must be dealt with, by shaming, slandering, vilifying, denigrating, lying, intimidating, blackmailing, expulsion from social circles or establishments, and any other means legally (or illegally, if necessary) possible. The socialists are masters at using the above techniques to gain power. Sounds familiar in today's American politics or in society when it comes to the Democrats versus Republicans?

Hitler and NAZI-Socialists had many rivals. The older established parties acted more civilized, but the Socialist-Democrats and especially the German Communist party stopped at nothing, including murder. The NAZI-Socialists were the opposition, the enemy to the other socialist parties. They coveted the same segment of the population as the Democratic-Socialists and the Communists. The increase in NAZI-Socialist membership and in Hitler's audiences attracted the attention of the Communists, who sent their Roter Frontkämpferbund (Red Front Fighters League) to break up the meetings. The Red Front Fighters resembled, down to the uniform and clubs, the Cheka of the Russian Bolshevik police organization.

Hitler responded by establishing his own paramilitary units, the Sturmabteilung (Storm Detachment) and the infamous SA or the brown shirts. At the beginning, they acted as security to protect against the communist attacks, but soon, after recruiting disgruntled veterans, the SA increased in number, up to two million by 1934. The members of the SA were recruited for being thugs, not scholars. Under the command of Ernst Rohm, they became a truly paramilitary force, Hitler's army. Through vehement and violent acts, the SA intimidated the non-participants, beating and terrorizing or even killing the Marxist-Socialist followers. The Red Front Fighters did the same against the NAZIs or any other opponents.

As a propaganda tool, the SA acted as demonstrators, marching through cities led by a band, NAZI-Socialist flags waving, leaflets distributed to the people, cars with megaphones mounted on top blaring the NAZI-Socialist doctrine, penetrating through every door and window. It was an impressive show of force by NAZI-Socialism. Power, or even perceived power, attracts new recruits and weakens the opposition.

Who conducts brutal actions at conservative rallies in the United States? Antifa, whose members, in spite of the group's name, *Anti-Fascism*, are no different from the NAZI SA brutes. And who are the members of Antifa? White people. They claim to be anti-fascists, but for sure they are NAZI-Socialists—even if they don't realize it.

Besides physical attacks, the liberals (Marxists in reality) are bent on destroying anyone of any influence who speaks against them. They do it by shaming, slandering, vilifying, denigrating, lying, intimidating, expelling them from social circles or establishments, and firing them from their jobs. If you value your reputation and job, you had better not utter anything politically incorrect or any conservative thought on Twitter or Facebook. You had better not wear anything with symbols that might upset the leftists. And definitely don't say anything or make movies that might infuriate China. And God help you if you show disrespect for Black Lives Matter by not taking a knee!

9.10. Absorb or Cannibalize Members from Other Parties.

To exist as a viable political party you need members, just as a religion needs worshipers. The more members a party has, the more money it has, because preaching on an empty stomach is not inspiring.

To enlarge his party membership:

> Hitler gave explicit instructions that all political affiliations were welcome in the NSDAP, and communists, social democrats, centrists, and moderate conservatives all deserted their parties to muster under the swastika.
> As Jonathan Meades puts it, the Third Reich was "a golden age for the joiner-in, the sycophant, and the sneak." [4: Munich – Speech of April 12, 1922]

This phenomenon occurred increasingly as the NAZI-Socialism movement was winning at the ballot boxes after 1928. Even people that did not have a preference politically joined the party, to belong with the other NAZI believers. What is more surprising is that the Marxists, socialists or communists, did not see much difference between the Marxism-Socialism and Nazi-Socialism. They both proclaimed to elevate the status of the people. As a bonus, the National-Socialists were nationalists not Internationalists as the Marxists were. In the book "The Big Lie" by Dinesh D'Souza the author quotes a situation that happened all too often in Germany, socialists and communists joining the National-Socialist party. On man showed his attic-shrine where he had NAZI paraphernalia of flags, posters, statues, pamphlets, and soon. A month before joining the National-Socialist, his shrine was adorned with communist paraphernalia of communist flags, hammer and sickle, Lenin posters and other memorabilia. Why did he switch? The men saw no ideological difference between Marxism-Socialism and National-Socialism.

When Hitler joined the German Worker's Party (DAP) movement, he was designated member number seven at the local level. Nationally, in the DAP, he had number 555, but the count started at 500 to give the impression that the movement had larger membership than it had. From fifty-five members in 1919, when Hitler joined, NAZI-Socialism had increased to 55,000 members by 1923, right before his Putsch. After he was imprisoned, the membership decreased by half, but by 1929, it had gone up to 130,000. By 1932, the membership reached 450,000. Although there were members who had never participated in any party before, many more came from the ranks of other parties as NAZI-Socialism increased in popularity.

The nationalist parties were prime candidates for recruiting, and even the German Socialist party members, realizing that there wasn't much difference between Marxist-Socialism and Nationalist-Socialism joined in.

In the US we have two major parties, the Democrats with forty-five million members and the Republicans with thirty-two million members. There is a third bloc of voters, the Independents, with thirty-one million. Cannibalizing members is not as important as convincing the independents and the opposition to vote for one party or another.

9.11. Enter Politics

After the 1923 Putsch, with Hitler in prison, the NAZI-Socialist party was briefly banned, but it participated in the elections of May 1924 under the National Socialist Freedom Party, winning thirty-two seats in the Reichstag, but the same year, in December 1924, after another election, that party lost eighteen seats and held onto only fourteen.

The punitive payments made to the winners of the Great War and then the financial policy of the Weimer government led to hyperinflation causing great resentment among Germans. During the hyperinflation years, the people had to carry money by wheelbarrow to buy a loaf of bread. Hyperinflation wiped out the wealth and savings of most middle-class Germans. That situation provided new fuel for the nationalist movement, and their membership increased considerably, fueled by the propaganda of Hitler, until the Putsch.

In 1929, the economic situation worsened in Germany. The Great Depression had begun, and millions of Germans were unemployed, a perfect situation and a great opportunity for the NAZI-Socialist party or any other party with the right formula. Extraordinary times provide extraordinary circumstances to be taken advantage of.

Germany had many political parties, some on the left, some in the center, some on the right, but none strong enough to guide Germany to recovery and prosperity. The Socialist-Democratic and Communist parties, as Marxist parties, had an internationalist agenda. All nationalities were equal and should follow Karl Marx's cry that the *world proletariat unite*. In other words, Germans, French, English, and all other nationalities, including the "despicable Jews," were brothers. But that was not the belief of a Nationalist-Socialist like Hitler and many other Germans.

Hitler Was a Socialists

The NSDAP, NAZI-Socialist, party was eventually legalized, and Hitler was allowed to speak in public, increasing again the membership of the party. It ran under its own name, NSDAP, for elections in 1928, obtaining only twelve seats in the Reichstag. Five years later, in 1933, after several other elections, the NAZI-Socialist party won 288 seats in the Reichstag, gaining at the expense of every party, including the Socialist-Democratic party, except for the German Communist Party. Additionally, eleven million more voters participated in the election for a total of seventeen million people casting their votes for the NAZI-Socialist party, in contrast with the 1928 election, when they had received only 810,000 votes. The National-Socialist propaganda appealed to the largest segment of the German people, although the party didn't achieve a majority in the Reichstag, denying Hitler the chancellorship.

How did Hitler achieve this kind of success? By exploiting the inability of the other parties to lift the economy from the Great Depression and reduce unemployment. There were six million unemployed in Germany, and the only party that brought a glimmer of hope, by promising everything to everyone, was the NAZI-Socialist party. Promises are easy to make, and Hitler, like all politicians, did not give out many details on how he would achieve what he promised. But being elected was what mattered.

In the USA we've experienced financial times comparable to those experienced during the Weimar Republic. Supposedly we don't have inflation, but with a national debt of $24 trillion in 2020, a GDP of $21 trillion, and a revenue of $3.7 trillion, one wonders. (The figures may be different at the end of 2020 depending on the economic situation affected by China-Wuhan Coronavirus pandemic.) Based on current conditions, how fast can we recover from the pandemic? And then how will the debt affect our economy? Stormy economic and political weather is ahead of us.

9.12.   Raise Money

In the beginning, as a political movement, the money for the NAZI-Socialists came mostly from membership fees and newspaper sales. The local chapters would meet in the local beer halls, and for the price of a stein of beer, they had a meeting hall. But as the movement grew, more money was necessary for propaganda, for meeting places larger than beer halls, for paying the cadres that were necessary to manage and organize the nascent party. Maintaining the SA cost lots of money, and although most foot soldiers were volunteers, it cost money to dress them, transport them, feed them, and organize parades and marches.

To enter politics, the NAZI-Socialist party needed bigger amounts of money. The membership fees, even as the headcount rose, could not provide such funds. Money to support the party and its political aspirations, including a plane to fly Hitler from city to city to give speeches, came from other deep pockets. Unlike the Communist German Party, which had monetary support from Moscow or extortion money from the industrialists to avoid strikes, the NAZI-Socialists did not have a rich uncle and did not want to antagonize the industrialists. They had support from other well-to-do nationalists, but not enough to provide the amount of money Hitler needed. There were a lot of industrialists who were fearful of Marxist-Socialism and the Communists. Hitler conducted a shrewd campaign. In public, he blasted the capitalists, the bankers, the financiers, and the nobility to appeal to the masses; but in private, behind closed doors, he was giving different speeches. It was well known that NAZI-Socialism was against Marxist-Socialism and Communism; therefore, the sell to the deep-pocket capitalists was easy.

Hitler, in so many words, gave the industrialists a choice: Pay me and I will destroy the Marxist-Socialists and Communists and their grasp on the unions. Or be at their mercy. Furthermore, Hitler promised that he would not expropriate property, as the Marxist-Socialists and Communists were determined to do. And the money rolled in. Besides donations, many of these industrialists also joined the party. What better way to keep an eye on their investment? Because of the intense and relentless campaigns, there was a time when the NAZI-Socialist party was near insolvency, but then, after Hitler pressed the industrialists for more, the money materialized. Private donations were needed until the party captured enough seats in the Reichstag. Once Hitler became the chancellor, and for subsequent elections, the money was supplied by the government. All the government assets were at the disposal of the NAZI-Socialist party for their political benefit.

The Bolsheviks, just like the German Communist Party, did not obtain their money from rich donors, at least not voluntarily. Joseph Stalin was one of the leading Bolshevik bank robbers and an extortionist, making sure that the party had enough resources for propaganda, newspapers, and weapons to conduct acts of sabotage and weaken the existing government in Russia prior to the 1917 revolution. According to Wikipedia information:

> [Stalin] . . . raised funds for Vladimir Lenin's Bolshevik faction via robberies, kidnappings, and protection rackets.
>
> Stalin organized the robbing of a large delivery of money to the Imperial Bank in June 1907. His gang ambushed the armed convoy in Yerevan Square with gunfire and homemade bombs. Around forty people were killed, but all of his gang escaped alive.
>
> In Baku he had reassembled his gang, the Outfit, and raised finances by running protection rackets, counterfeiting currency, and carrying out robberies. They also kidnapped the children of several wealthy figures to extract ransom money.

Money is the blood of every political and revolutionary cause, and it must be obtained in whatever way to maintain a viable movement. Who finances the Neo-Marxist-Leninist Black Lives Matter? George Soros financed it at first, but after BLM became a major political force, the money came from the political sympathizers in Hollywood and from pressuring businesses to "donate" for a "just cause."

9.13. Elections

The purpose of all these efforts was to acquire political power in the legislative body through elections. Hitler had learned after his Putsch that Germany was not Italy. It would be difficult to acquire power as easily as Mussolini did. He also knew that Germany was not Russia, grabbing power through armed revolution, although some members in his party structure, especially Ernst Rohm and the SA, were ready to start a bloody revolution to seize total power. Hitler promised that he would gain power only through fair, popular elections. While at the same time, he always claimed that he wanted complete political power to achieve his dreams.

Germany had state legislatures called the Landtag and a federal body, similar to the US Congress, called the Reichstag. After entering into politics and running for seats in the Reichstag, the success of NSDAP was meteoric. The results in German national elections from 1928 and 1933 to the Reichstag were as follows:

Party	1928 Votes	Seats	1933 Votes	Seats
KPD	3,265	54	4,848	81
SPD	9,153	153	7,181	120
Centre	3,712	61	4,425	74
BVP	946	17	1,074	18
DDP	1,479	25	334	5
WP	1,388	23	0	0
DVP	2,680	45	432	2
DNVP	4,382	73	3,137	52
NSDAP	**810**	**12**	**17,277**	**288**

(Votes are in thousands and do not represent the total votes for all the minor parties participating in the elections.) Source: Wikipedia

How do the results compare between the Marxist-Socialists parties KPD (communists), SPD (socialists) and the DNVP (German National People's) versus NSDAP (NAZI-Socialism)? The NAZI-Socialist party gained at everyone else's expense. NAZI-Socialism was more appealing to the German people than the international socialism of the Socialist and Communist parties. Hitler also conducted a relentless campaign during both the election and off-election cycle.

Chapter 10. Acquire Total Power

Total political power can be achieved through legal or fraudulent elections, through revolution or coup-d'état. Even the Bolsheviks were elected to the Duma of Russia in 1912, but being in a minority and unable to achieve any changes of their liking, they acted on a coup d'état in 1917. In the aftermath of the coup d'état, the Bolsheviks occupied the Winter Palace in St. Petersburg, took the Tsar and his family prisoners, and the October Revolution began, taking advantage of a Russia weakened by the World War I. The bloody revolution, à la Bolshevik 1917 October style, can be accomplished only in times of complete anarchy and weakness of the government, just as in China after the end of the WWII.

In times of peace, in a country that, although in bad shape, is not in disarray, a bloody revolution is almost impossible to carry out. Hitler tried a putsch (coup-d'état,) à la Mussolini, in 1923, to take over the Bavarian government and failed. Afterwards, he realized that without support of the military, any revolution would be squashed.

The Bolsheviks were the first to meet the Russian soldiers returning from the front and convince them to join their cause, thereby assuring their revolution's success. Fighting against the revolution, the entrenched political powers will use the military to prevent and overcome the revolutionaries. In the case of Russia, many of those returning from the front took the side of the Bolsheviks.

In the book *Hitler* Joachim C. Fest says:

> Consequently, it was Hitler who created the modern concept of revolution. . ... Modern revolution . . . did not overcome power but "seized" it, and employed bureaucratic rather than bellicose methods. It was a quiet process. . ... This revolution reached deep and spared nothing. It gripped and changed the political institutions, shattered the class structures in the army, the bureaucracy, and to some extent the economy. It broke up, corrupted, and enfeebled the still influential nobility and the old upper crust. In a Germany that owed its charm as well as its provinciality to the same backwardness, it introduced that degree of social mobility and egalitarianism indispensable to a modern industrial society. [2]

Hitler and the NAZI-Socialist party obtained the largest bloc of seats in the Reichstag in the 1932 and 1933 elections, but still not a majority. He could not become the chancellor without a majority vote in the Reichstag and the acceptance of President Hindenburg. But everything is possible in politics if you know how. And Hitler did know how.

Hitler convinced former Chancellor Franz von Papen and, with the help of President Hindenburg, ousted Chancellor Kurt von Schleicher. Hitler became the chancellor on January 30, 1933, with Franz von Papen as vice-chancellor. Von Papen thought that he and other cabinet appointees would control Hitler. Little did they know! The new chancellor, Adolf Hitler, asked for only two ministerial positions in his cabinet, that of Minister of the Interior for Prussia for Hermann Goering and Minister of the Interior of Germany (the police) for Wilhelm Frick. The other ministerial positions were held by the other coalition parties, reassuring themselves that Hitler was under their control. How naive of them to think they could control Hitler! He had two dedicated NAZIs in charge of the police, a very important step for acquiring complete political power, *and* he had some military support.

Hitler set up another election for March 5, 1933, hoping to obtain a clear majority. On February 27, the Reichstag burned down, and the arsonist was allegedly Marinus van der Lubbe, a Dutch Communist. Much later it was suspected that Goering had orchestrated the event. The burning of the Reichstag prompted the issuance of the Enabling Act of 1933, which gave Chancellor Hitler the power to enact laws without a Reichstag vote. Hitler wasted no time outlawing the German Communist Party, a deadly adversary. After the election of March 5, 1933, Hitler and the NAZI-Socialist party gained more seats in the Reichstag, but still not a majority. He then formed a coalition with the German National People's Party and eventually outmaneuvered this coalition to become a dictator. The road was open for him alone to make all decisions and transform democratic Germany into a one-party NAZI-Socialist Germany.

After gaining dictatorial power Hitler answered those who accused him of being a dictator as follows:

> "I am not a dictator and never will be a dictator," he declared and added rather contemptuously: "As a dictator any clown can govern." He had, he admitted, eliminated the principle of democratic voting, but that by no

> means meant that he was free; strictly speaking, no such thing as arbitrary rule existed, only various ways of expressing the "general will." He solemnly assured his listeners: "National Socialism is the true realization of democracy, which has degenerated under parliamentarianism. . .. We have cast aside outmoded institutions precisely because they no longer served to keep in fruitful contact with the totality of the nation, because they led to idle chatter, to impudent cheating." [2: pg 418]

What a master of deception! And considering that he had obtained his dictatorial power with almost full support of the Reichstag, who could argue with him? President Hindenburg died, and Hitler combined the offices of the president and the chancellor. He even put his appointment to the test of elections in a plebiscite on August 19, 1934, for which he received 88% of the German vote for the merger of the two offices. To top it all off, his "dictatorial" appointment was for only four years, after which the German people would get to vote again to keep him in power. He obtained all his powers *democratically*. Of course, before the next election opponents disappear, and censorship and propaganda alter the citizen's perception of being led by the one and only Adolf Hitler and his NAZI-Socialist party.

After another accusation of being a dictator, in a speech of January 30, 1937, in the Reichstag, he said:

> There is now only one representative of German sovereignty—the people itself. [4]

In the meantime, the NAZI-Socialist party membership swelled. Besides the die-hard earlier followers, a new wave of idealists joined. As by now Hitler's speeches could be heard everywhere, a new wave of opportunists also joined in. The newly created government jobs went to the NAZI-Socialist members first. As for those people who did not vote for the NAZI-Socialist party, the party knew who they were as the ballots, although secret, were not so secret, and Goering's Gestapo had a long list of dissenters to deal with soon after the election.

It took Hitler a little over a year to obtain dictatorial power and change Germany into a NAZI-Socialist state. Lenin, on the other hand, after the October 1917 revolution, had to fight a civil war against the Whites in Russia for many years before achieving complete control over the country by 1923.

Socialist Hitler's attack on democracy and his success in eliminating democracy should serve as a warning to us here in the United States. How popular is the Congress nowadays? The ratings are in the teens, which is abominable for an elected body. Sure, we can vote them out of power and replace them with new legislators, but they'll continue the same shenanigans as before. Were you surprised when the people revolted and voted for a non-politician for president, for Donald Trump? He is not a threat to democracy in spite of what the leftist and fake-news media say.

The threat to democracy will be the Democrat-Socialist party, with killer instincts, with a majority and complete control of both houses of Congress, making use of the Democrat party control of most of the media and the leftist deep-state bureaucrats willing to assist, possibly, President Joe Biden and his ultra-leftist V.P. Kamala Harris could cause the *perfect storm* by suspending the constitution based on economic/financial/social disturbance reasons.

How does the situation look in the summer of 2020 with a pandemic, high unemployment, economic slowdown, and BLM/Antifa rioting in the streets? The November 2020 election is that perfect-storm moment. Joe Biden may not be that man, but he is replaceable, by his V.P. Kamala Harris and other manipulators.

10.1 Eliminate the Opposition

Invoking the Enabling Act of 1934, and after the death of President Hindenburg, Hitler moved quickly to declare Germany a one-party state, the National Socialist Germany. All other parties were outlawed, and anyone who presented a problem was incarcerated. Later, the detainees were sent to concentration camps.

As for internal opposition in the NSDAP, Hitler, like Stalin, learned well from Machiavelli that achieving power and maintaining power are different and that maintaining power might not be feasible with the same rabble-rousers that brought him into power. In 1934, on the Night of the Long Knives, Hitler disposed of his paramilitary forces, the SA's leadership. The SA had served its function and, the moment Hitler achieved dictatorial powers, was no longer needed. At the same time, he also disposed of his rivals in the NSDAP party, clearing the path to control the NAZI-Socialist party without opposition.

Stalin acted similarly in the Soviet Union during the terror years of 1936–38, when he purged his military and political opponents within the Communist party and in the intelligentsia.

Hitler Was a Socialists

Referring to politics, in *Mein Kampf*, Hitler said:

> The longer a man possesses an object the more readily he grows tired of it. He craves something new: therefore one needs two parties. One in the office, the other in opposition. When the one has played itself out, then the opposition party comes in power. . ..As everyone knows, this system is given some such name as "Self-Government of the People." [5]

When the people get tired of one party and want change, they vote for the opposition party. Through democracy, one can achieve political power, but it is the way to lose it as well. That was not the way to govern and accomplish his ideals. Democracy is weak, as it was in the Weimar Republic, and Hitler tailored his propaganda to appeal to the dissatisfied German people to get the political power. To Hitler there was only one way to govern, through State control, Socialist Dictatorship.

This sounds awfully similar to the United States system of government, very apropos of the American political parties today: the Republican and the Democrat parties. The political revolving door ushers one party into power, while the other one is in opposition. Meanwhile, nothing gets done.

When it comes to opposition, in *The Black Book of Communism* Mikhail Tomsky, the leader of the Soviet trade unions, stated:

> We allow other parties to exist. However, the fundamental principle that distinguishes us from the West is as follows: one party rules, and all others are in jail! [9: pg 7]

Most likely dead, I may add.

10.2   Control the Media

Information is power—power to influence, persuade, or threaten. If you have the mouthpiece, you have their ears. Media in those days were mostly the press, radio, or cinema newsreels. The Nazi-Socialist party had its own paper, the *Völkischer Beobachter*. All the leftist newspapers were shut down and their editors thrown in prison. The Jewish publications were all confiscated. There were some newspapers of the center and right that were allowed to stay in business. After all, NAZI-Socialist Germany was a democratic country under the people's leadership. The papers that were allowed to be published fell under the control of Joseph Goebbels, the Minister of Propaganda. His ministry censored all papers or fed them the news that was in line with the NAZI-Socialist party line. The editors had to be *racially clean* German citizens, definitely not Jewish or married to Jews. The radio and cinema were under his complete control. Goebbels had at his disposal all the means to spread the "good news" or blast enemies. One of the slogans was *Gemeinnutz vor Eigennutz* (The Common Interest Before Self) that incentivized the Germans to do everything for Germany. In practice, the higherups in the NAZI-Socialist party were lining their pockets—as is always the case.

Stalin started the "Stakhanovite movement" to honor a Hero of Socialist Labor, Andrei Stakhanov, who was a Russian Soviet miner. He heroically outperformed his fellow miners and challenged his coworkers to outperform him. Copper medals were awarded aplenty, but not a kopek (penny) in bonuses, à la Communist-Socialist style.

10.3 Control the Police

As was shown earlier, before obtaining dictatorial powers, Hitler insisted on only two appointments to his cabinet, the Interior Ministry of the Reich and the police for Prussia. Having control of the police, Hitler could move with impunity against the other Marxist-Socialist parties, which he did, and any other dissidents that stood in his way.

Every Socialist state needs secret police to protect the government from its people. And so the infamous Gestapo (*Geheime Staatspolizei*, the Secret Police) was formed in 1933 by Hermann Goering, and in 1934 Heinrich Himmler became its chief. The role of the Gestapo was to get rid of (arrest, torture, extract information from, murder) anyone opposing the NAZI-Socialist State.

The Soviet Union's equivalent organization was the NKVD, which acted as regular police *and* secret service to annihilate dissidents. Later, in East Germany, the organization equivalent to the Gestapo or the NKVD was the *Stasi*, the State Security Service, which controlled and terrorized the East German people. Based on the NKVD template, all the other Communist-Socialist states had similar organizations, including the *Securitate* in

Romania, which caused every Romanian to freeze with fear when its name was whispered. One of their agents was part of the "interrogation team" at my school investigating my minor rebellion against the system when I was a teenager. I describe this in *Escape from Communism*.

The Gestapo had a force of 7,500 officers in NAZI-Socialist Germany for a population of eighty million people. NKVD had a force of 306,000[9] in Communist-Socialist Soviet Union for a population of 168 million people. The comparison is based on 1939 statistics. This ratio may not be a fair comparison because the Germans were content with NAZI-Socialism, they were voted into power, while the Bolsheviks took over Russia at the gun point, and the Russian people had experienced Communism-Socialism for twenty years by then and also the famines and the red terror years of the mid-1930s. In a socialist country the worst it gets the more secret police is needed.

The Gestapo is described in *How Socialist Was National Socialism* as follows:

> The German people did not fear the Gestapo as much as he needed to fear what his neighbors might tell the Gestapo.
>
> Pressure to conform from above, and fear of non-conformity below, combined to produce a claustrophobic, suffocating environment in which each person's every word and deed was under the closest scrutiny, even within families.
> [8]

Indeed, just as in Communist-Socialist Romania, there were informants everywhere, and just one word whispered to *Securitate* and you regretted you were born. There is no such fear in the United States, unless you voice a politically incorrect thought on Twitter and get fired, or someone accuses you of sexual harassment without proof, and your career is in ruins.

All the state secret-police organizations in Socialist states are responsible for political crimes, internal or external. Which organization will triumph in a future United Socialists of America? FBI, the Secret Service, or yet a new organization to be selected from the most devoted socialists?

10.4. Control the Military

The purge of 1934 represented another important goal for Hitler. Previously, although he was able to politically control the government, he didn't have the allegiance of the military, which was all-important to his future plans for Russia. The SA leader, Ernst Rohm, was not happy with the political solution the NAZI-Socialists achieved under Hitler and pushed for a complete revolution to reshape Germany. He also wanted to integrate the SA, two million strong, into the military. That was not acceptable to the military hierarchy, most of whom were officers of noble descent. Hitler removed the SA objection the military had and, as commander in chief, obtained their total allegiance.

However, the military hierarchy was firmly entrenched and, at times of weakness, could rebel against the Führer. There were many generals who plotted against Hitler. To tighten his control of the Wehrmacht in 1938, he ousted Generals Werner von Blomberg and Werner von Fritsch and appointed Wilhelm Keitel, who, as the Chief of the Armed Forces High Command, was Hitler's man. Hitler had the army take a personal oath of allegiance to him.

Unlike Germany with a reduced military of just 100,000, most of whom were officers, Stalin had a large military with many officers from the old regime or with old allegiances. He made sure that he obtained the allegiance of the military through mass executions of the officer corps, crippling his army at the beginning of World War II.

10.5. Take Over the Unions

Trade unions were the stronghold of Communists and Democratic-Socialists. The NAZI-Socialists tried to infiltrate the unions but with lukewarm success. Most unions didn't believe that NAZI-Socialists were actually proworker. To consolidate his power, Hitler had to control the unions, as they could organize general strikes and cripple his rearmament of Germany. May Day was an official German holiday, and Hitler had adopted it fully. He even renamed it the Day of National Labor and prepared a grand celebration, inviting all trade union representatives to attend. Hitler came up with the motto "Honor work and respect the worker," promising that May Day would be celebrated for a long time.

The next day, on May 2, 1933, all union headquarters were occupied by the SS. The unions were dissolved, the leaders thrown in prison, and their funds confiscated. A new all-encompassing union, the German Labor Front, was formed under the leadership of Dr. Robert Lay. And so, without firing a shot, all independent unions became one NAZI-Socialist union. The workers were promised even better days ahead, and the business sector was satisfied that Hitler kept his promise to tame the unions. Under the German Labor Front, collective bargaining was abolished, and new party appointees took over all the important positions.

Similarly, in the Soviet Union, and later in all the European Communist-Socialist countries, the independent unions were incorporated under one state union, and the communist party controlled the unions. Under Communism-Socialism, the unions became company unions and were organized by factory rather than by trade. Every factory had a union under the umbrella of the All-Union Central Council, and its members did not communicate with members from other factories, preventing them from uniting. The union gave the workers a place to voice their opinions or grievances, be indoctrinated in the Marxist-Leninist cause, and keep an eye out for troublemakers.

In contrast, in the United States as in other democratic countries, the unions are organized by trade, like the United Auto Workers or the Teamsters, and the workers are employed by different companies.

10.6. The Leader's Image

By definition, a dictator is the *supreme leader*, and everyone *must* idolize him. I lived under one such dictator, Nicolae Ceausescu, and his pictures were everywhere, including every classroom. Everyone giving political speeches had to laud the great "conductor," the Führer, to a point that became nauseating. In the later years of his dictatorship, any book published in Romania had to have a quote from him at the beginning of the book. Of course, they were not Ceausescu's words but those of some writer spewing worthless communist propaganda.

I'm sure you saw on TV how the North Koreans *adore* their leader Kim Jong-Un. They applaud enthusiastically with hands raised high and smiles, smiles, smiles, while their bellies protest in hunger.

Hitler worked hard at polishing his image as a leader, and claimed:

> All my life I have been a "have-not." At home I was a "have-not." I regard myself as belonging to them and have always fought exclusively for them. I defended them and, therefore, I stand before the world as their representative."
>
> Owing to the peculiar circumstances of my life I am perhaps more capable than anyone else of understanding and realizing the nature and the whole life of the various German castes. Not because I've been able to look down on this life from above but because I have participated in it, because I stood in the midst of this life, because fate in a moment of caprice or perhaps fulfilling the designs of Providence, cast me into the great mass of people, amongst common folk. Because I myself was a laboring man for

years in the building trade and had to earn my own bread. And because for a second time I took my place once again as an ordinary soldier amongst the masses and because then life raised me into strata of our people so that I know these, too, better than countless others who were born in these strata. So fate has perhaps fitted me more than any other to be the broker—I think I may say—the honest broker for both sides alike. Here I am not personally interested; I am not dependent upon the state or any other public office; I am not dependent upon business or industry or any trade union. I am an independent man, and I have set before myself no other goal than to serve, to best of my power and ability, the German people, and above all to serve the millions who, thanks to their simple trust and ignorance and thanks to the baseness of their former leaders have perhaps suffered more than any other class. [4: Berlin, Rheinmetall-Borsig Works – Speech December 10, 1940]

The Führer is one of us, the downtrodden, and he has our interest at heart. How, therefore, could you not *idolize* such a man? Everywhere you turned, you saw his face. Might as well surrender and accept his supreme leadership—or the Gestapo will be standing by to *help*.

According to Joachim C. Fest, Hitler cultivated his image as follows:

Myth of the man from the people.
Unknown frontline soldier in the First World War.
Man without name, without money, without influence, without a following.
Thus he likes to have resplendent uniforms around him, for they pointed up to the

simplicity of his own costume. His air of
unassuming austerity and soberness, together
with his unwedded state and his withdrawn life,
could be splendidly fused in the public mind
into the image of a great, solitary man bearing
the burden of his election by destiny, marked
by the mystery of self-sacrifice. [2: pg 521]

And as a dictator, he was a democratic, socialist dictator
as Hitler said in one of his speeches:

So great was the Revolution that its spiritual
foundations have not been understood even
today by a superficial world. They speak of
democracies and dictatorships, and have not
realized that in this country a Revolution has
taken place that can be described as democratic
in the highest sense of the word. Does a more
glorious *socialism* or a truer democracy exist
than that which enables any German boy to find
his way to the head of the nation? The purpose
of the Revolution was not to deprive a
privileged class of its rights, but to raise a class
without rights to equality. [4: Berlin, Reichstag –
Speech January 30, 1937] Emphasis added.

This is one of the distinctions between Marxism-
Socialism and National-Socialism. Under Marxism, a
certain class of people is eliminated so that everyone is
reduced to the lowest common denominator, the
proletariat. Hitler inspired his followers by elevating
everyone from the lowest common denominator to the
higher classes. How was he going to accomplish his
promises? By invading other lands.

During his dictatorship, people saluted each other with
"Heil Hitler!" and a raised hand in the Fascist, old Roman

salute. His pictures hung everywhere along with NAZI-Socialist flags and the swastika. Germany became Hitler's Germany.

Identical leader worship occurred in the Soviet Union for Joseph Stalin, in Communist China for Mao Zedong, and in Vietnam for Ho Chi Minh. And let's not forget our *beloved campanero*, Cuba's Fidel Castro.

Statues, on the other hand, are reserved for the dead leaders like Kim Il-Sung of North Korea or Vladimir Ilyich Lenin, who even has a statue adorned with flowers in the state of Washington while our founding father's statue, George Washington, had our American flag burned on his face and his statue toppled down. These are the works of the Socialists of America.

Of course, the mummies of Lenin and Ho Chi Minh and Mao are displayed in superior reverence, transforming their corporeal personas into those of *gods*.

Gods who killed millions of people.

10.7.   Disarm the Population

In the years before he came to power Hitler said:
> We called on the masses of the people not to surrender their arms, for the surrender of one's arms would be nothing less than the beginning of enslavement. [4: Munich, Speech April 12, 1922]

If he were to start a revolution, his SA and an armed population was much needed. As a matter of fact, his SA stormtroopers were armed and used their arms to instill fear and even to kill the dissenters and the opposition.

129

Allegedly, Lenin very *wisely* said:
One man with a gun can control 100 without one.

He who has the guns controls the population. No Communist-Socialist country allowed the population to own guns. Sure, they could have hunting guns, which were held at the police station during off-season. And after you fired your gun, you had better bring back the empty shells, accounting for every bullet. For a private citizen, owning a handgun was punishable by decades in prison.

After Hitler came to power and after the purge of 1934, dissolving the SA to prevent them from starting a bloody revolution, he took actions to disarm the population. An armed population is a danger to any totalitarian government and especially to a socialist government. I remember a while ago seeing a propaganda poster of Hitler holding the hands of a boy and girl and urging the people to surrender their guns. Why should the people be armed? Adolf Hitler and the National Socialist State would protect them.

The first people to be disarmed were the Jews. The Nazis prevented them from employment, closing their shops and businesses, and after that the Jews had no way to revolt, especially on Kristallnacht, or the Night of Broken Glass, in 1938 when the Nazis marauded the streets, smashing windows of Jewish-owned shops and buildings and burning down synagogues.

Full disarmament of German population did not happen. The war made it irrelevant when so many Germans were drafted and armed for war.

10.8. Religion

Religion is the biggest enemy of a totalitarian government, unless it *is* the government. For socialist atheists, Marxism-Leninism is their religion, and any religion with a god is barely tolerated. Sure, Lenin paid lip service to the church as independent and having no part in the Soviet government, but that was at the beginning when the Bolsheviks did not need more enemies. Stalin, however, did not spare religion, and he demolished many churches trying to diminish the power of the church. The population's heart can be either with God or with the Communist-Socialist party.

Hitler was a Catholic by birth, and at first, he didn't make the church, Catholics *or* Protestants, an issue. Judaism was another matter. In NAZI-Socialist Germany, the party members were able to kill Jews and go to church without any contradiction. Hitler portrayed his party as a Christian party and unlike other politicians during the Weimar Republic he did not enter in coalitions with the Marxist parties. As he said in his speeches:

> And now Staatsprasident Bolz says that Christianity and the Catholic faith are threatened by us. And to that charge I can answer: In the first place it is Christians and not internationalist atheists who now stand at the head of Germany . . . at no time was greater internal damage done to Christianity than in these fourteen years when a party, theoretically Christian, sat with those who denied God in one

131

and the same government. [4: Stuttgart – Speech February 15, 1933]

Like all socialists, Hitler had the same problem with religions. They criticized him and lowered his status. And, of course, the people's mind can be with God or with the National Socialist party, but God did not count when Hitler was present.

He understood that changing the hearts of people when it came to politics or religion could not be carried out by force alone, but by offering a different alternative that is as compelling as the old one, he said:

> Any attempt to combat a philosophy with methods of violence will fail in the end, unless the fight takes the form of attack for a new spiritual attitude. Only in the struggle between two philosophies can the weapon of brutal force, persistently and ruthlessly applied, lead to a decision for the sake of the side it supports.
> [5: pg 172]

His philosophy was that National-Socialism had to be believed and adhered to as passionately as those of religion. But fighting a religion by force, would be futile. Countering an existing religion with another religion, as in National-Socialism, would succeed, and if necessary with the use of force.

Point 24 of the NAZI-Socialism Political Program stated:

> We want to allow all religions in the State, unless they offend the moral feelings of the German race. The NSDAP is Christian, but does not belong to any denomination.

At the beginning the religions were free to practice as long as they didn't stand against NAZI-Socialism. Later, Hitler attempted to eliminate the Old Testament from the

Bible for being of Jewish origin. Somehow he forgot that Jesus was Jewish, or maybe not, as he envisioned a new religion. Religious leaders who opposed him were thrown in prison or concentration camps.

Hitler envisioned a new religion, the National Reich Church of Germany. In an envisioned future, all religious symbols, including the crucifix, were to be removed from all churches and replaced by the swastika. On the altars of the new churches, *Mein Kampf* was to be the new Bible.

This is no different from what the Communist-Socialists tried to do: eliminate the church as an institution, except they didn't have a need to replace the crucifix with the hammer and sickle as the churches were not needed anymore. The people's mind is to be controlled by one entity alone: the one-party State, and its bible was the "Marxist-Leninist Manifesto".

Joachim Fest said that Adolf Hitler had grand plans for the Christian Church:

> After the end of war, when the great reckonings with the churches had begun and the Pope in tiara and full pontifical in St. Peter's Square had been hanged, Strasbourg Cathedral would be converted into a monument to the Unknown Soldier. [2]

I think the Communist-Socialists would proudly approve.

10.9. The Social Classes and the Rich

Social classes, monarchy, nobility, and the industrialists were the power structure of Germany of those days. You were either one of them or you were nothing. Per the Treaty of Versailles, monarchy was abolished, and a constitutional democracy was instituted. However, the nobility was thoroughly entrenched in the society. Unless you were a "Von," a Junker (the landed nobility of Prussia), a noble, you could not become an officer in the military. President Hindenburg often derided Hitler as "that Austrian corporal" and resisted assigning the chancellor position to him until he had no choice when Hitler held the largest political party bloc in the Reichstag.

Nobility and the elite held a dim view of Hitler and the NAZI-Socialist party. They were considered unlearned, brutish, and thugs, which they were. Indeed, in the beginning, the National-Socialist party was composed of veterans, peasants and working-class people. The upper classes preferred the status quo, tradition, privileges, which are barriers to any revolution, including the NAZI-Socialist revolution. Hitler didn't try to eliminate this class, but he bypassed it. This class was not in power anymore. That Austrian corporal, and as a socialist, opened up the society for everyone to participate to their best ability in politics, the military, or the economy. In one of his speeches he said:

> We recognize no classes, we see only the German people, millions of peasants, bourgeoisie, and workers, who will either overcome together the difficulties of these times or be overcome by them.
>
> There are no such things as classes: They cannot be . . . in Germany where everyone has the same blood, the same eyes and speaks the same language, here can be no class, here can be only a single people. [4: Berlin: Proclamation to the German Nation – February 1, 1933]

134

Hitler Was a Socialists

Although he was not of the nobility, claiming to be bourgeois, Hitler enjoyed being around nobility, especially women. The nobility had had the power in Germany, although it was eroded after the Great War. He indeed ignored the upper classes by not recognizing nobility as a minimum prerequisite to obtaining any function in the government. Now the prerequisite was to be a National-Socialist party member. But the titles and the classes remained, and the nobles were not eliminated or killed outright as happened in the Bolshevik Soviet Union, or all other Communist-Socialist countries.

Berlin, Reichstag Speech of January 30, 1937, Hitler said:

> We of this Government feel responsible for the restoration of orderly life in the nation and for the final elimination of class madness and class struggle.
>
> It is not only in ordinary life that we have succeeded in appointing the best among the people for every position . . . we have even succeeded in breaking down prejudice in a place where it was most deep-seated—in the fighting forces. Thousands of officers are being promoted from the ranks today. In this instance, too, we have overcome all social obstacles. [4: Berlin, Reichstag Speech of January 30, 1937]

Spoken like a true Marxist-Socialist—or any socialist.

When I grew up in Communist-Socialist Romania, part of the indoctrination was the hatred and elimination of the upper classes and the rich. They were the exploiters. My mother's family was wealthy, but they were not nobility, and they were not old rich but new rich, bourgeois. That may have saved them from deportation to the Romanian gulag. As far as their possessions, a lifetime of hard work, they were confiscated. The family was lucky to keep their house.

Hitler did not declare a war on the rich, as many of them helped NAZI-Socialism financially to come to power. Nor did he nationalize their assets. His goal was to implement socialism by acquiring other nations' wealth, not by internal redistribution of wealth as the Marxist-Socialist's manifesto dictates.

10.10.   Indoctrination and Education

Coming into power, acquiring total power, is not the end of the road as far as controlling the people's minds. Even in democracies, there is a certain amount of indoctrination, which we receive in schools or from media. People are fickle, and soon they'll get used to the current situation and want something new, or more. Or they wake up the morning after and realize what hellhole they were led into by voting for one party or another. Enthusiasm and blind following can be maintained only through constant indoctrination—continuous reaffirmation of how well we, the people, are served by the party in power.

Joachim Fest noted:

> Hitler was not exaggerating when he asserted that he asked his followers for nothing but sacrifices. In fact he had rediscovered the old truism that most people have a need for fitting into an organized whole, that there is joy in fulfilling a function, and that for the majority of the German people, the demand for selfless service frequently had a far greater appeal than

the intellectuals' demand of freedom for the individual. [2]

The above comment is very interesting, considering the following statement from *How "Socialist" Was National Socialism?*:

> People who escaped from communist East Germany complained about being compelled to conform, but then soon complained about their loneliness in the west. In either system, therefore, be it communist socialism or national socialism, the people were never free; they were always—in Hitler's words— "firmly fitted into discipline from which they [could not] escape," and conformity was the only realistic option. In this sense, NAZI Germany was every bit as socialist as its rivals in the USSR. [8]

Or all the other Communist-Socialist countries, for that matter: Keep their minds occupied, repeat the socialist slogans, don't let anyone wonder *what if.*

Joachim C. Fest better summarized the state of indoctrination Hitler maintained in Germany:

> In keeping with this view, the psychological mobilization of the country was not left to chance or whim, certainly not to the operations of dissent. It was the product of consistent, totalitarian penetration of all social structures by means of a close-knit system of supervision, regimentation, and guidance. The object was to "belabor people as long as necessary, until they succumb to us." That meant penetrating the private realm as well as every social area. "We must develop organizations in which an individual's entire life can take place. Then every activity and every need of every

> individual will be regulated by collectivity represented by the party. There is no longer any arbitrary will, there are no longer any free realms in which the individual belongs to himself." [2: pg 418]

In other words, complete control of the people's minds. This is what socialist serfdom is all about. This is George Orwell's *1984*, which all socialists aspire to achieve.

Part of the re-education of the population was to learn the proper NAZI-Socialist program, and many educational books were revised accordingly to reflect the "healthy" NAZI-Socialist philosophy. The NAZI-Socialists eliminated any books deemed subversive or ideologically contrary to the National-Socialist doctrine. Starting in 1933, the German Student Union conducted a campaign of book burning. In great ceremonies, in any large city plaza, at night, books were set afire. The books thrown in the fire were Jewish, Marxist, socialist, communist, pacifist, religious, liberal, anarchist and many others spreading "dangerous" knowledge. The Germans were a cultured and learned bunch, so there were a lot of books to dispose of.

In some of the Communist-Socialist countries, there were not enough books to round up and burn. All it took was a declaration of what dangerous books were illegal, and after a few arrests and beatings for owning antisocialist books, book owners burned the books themselves.

Rewriting books is standard procedure in any Socialist country. By rewriting history, elevating the revolutionary bank robbers and thieves (like Stalin) or social and political troublemakers to the status of heroes, while eliminating or discrediting the past heroes and the men who built the country. It is all intended to brainwash the people.

This is similar to what is happening in the United States today—removing statues of past heroes, eradicating the names of benefactors to society because they were slave owners, or renaming streets or plazas that were named after Columbus to whatever the new socialists think is politically correct, and rewriting the history of our country based on Neo-Marxist-Leninist beliefs.

The best time to achieve lasting indoctrination is when the mind is young, in school. Beyond indoctrination, the National-Socialists intended to shape every young person intellectually and physically into the new National-Socialist man or woman, as happened in NAZI Germany. As Hitler declared:

> This new Reich will give its youth to no one,
> but will itself take youth and give to youth its
> own education and its own upbringing. [3: pg 249]

The education will not be left to just anyone but only to the National-Socialist State.

Education from the first grade to university was nazified to fulfill Hitler's declaration. All teachers and professors had to join the National Socialist Teachers League, which was held "responsible for the execution of the ideological and political co-ordination of all teachers in accordance with the National Socialist Doctrine," [3] and were required to take an oath to "be loyal and obedient to Adolf Hitler." [3]

Hitler Youth schools eventually enrolled all young people in NAZI Germany with the following purpose:

> The German youth, besides being reared within
> the family and schools, shall be educated
> physically, intellectually and morally in the

spirit of National Socialism . . . through the
Hitler Youth. [3: pg 253]

If I take the above statement and rewrite it as follows:
*Our youth, besides being reared within the
family and schools, shall be educated
physically, intellectually and morally in the
spirit of Marxism-Leninism . . . through the
Communist Youth.*
The above statement is generically applicable to any
Communist-Socialist country in Europe. The kids, at least
in Communist-Socialist Romania, a carbon copy of Soviet
Union, had to join the organization called *Pioneers*
wearing red bandanas. Later, as teenagers, they graduated
to *UTC*, the Union of Teen Communists. Finally, they
would become full Communist Party members in order to
make use of the communist state benefits or to enter
colleges. Yes, I was one of those *Pioneers* and a *UTC*
member. There was no choice if I wanted schooling from
the Communist-Socialist State or did not want my parents
visited by the dreaded *Securitate*. Unfortunately, I was a
slow learner or hardheaded and the communist-socialist
doctrine never stuck. All my naturally born instincts told
me Communism-Socialism was wrong and evil.

Unlike Communist-Socialist countries, where the
schools were governed by the socialist state and the
Communist Party under strict rules and a rigid curriculum,
in NAZI-Socialist Germany, at first, there were other
private and parochial schools, and not all kids were
enrolled in Hitler's youth program. However, by 1939, all
kids had to be enrolled in Hitler Youth, unless the parents
wanted to be arrested by the Gestapo for a sobering
experience.

Hitler Was a Socialists

One may wonder why Nazism had very little opposition from the population when shortages appeared before the World War II. By then, the new National-Socialist men and women were part of the society.

As Hitler said:

> When an opponent declares, "I will not come over to your side," I calmly say, "Your child belongs to us already. . .. What are you? You will pass on. Your descendants, however, now stand in the new camp. In short time they will know nothing else but this new community." [3: pg 249]

Apparently, Hitler's socialist "cousin" Lenin was of a similar opinion:

> Give us the child for 8 years and it will be a Bolshevik forever.

Lenin was wrong. The Communist-Socialist schooling I received in Romania for eleven years had the opposite effect on me. All that socialist stuff was wasted on me, and I did not appreciate the equality of socialist serfdom.

Another purpose of socialist schools was to have the kids spy on their parents for subversive activities or anti-socialist talk at home. This happened in NAZI-Socialist Germany and in the other Communist-Socialist countries. In the USSR, a thirteen-year-old boy, Pavel Morozov, became a national hero when he denounced his father for anti-communist activities. The father was executed. Tragically, the kid's family killed him for what he did, and his family in turn was executed as well. After that, Pavel Morozov became a martyr of the USSR. Imagine what any parent would think or do after reading in the communist papers about what happened. You wouldn't dare to talk ill of the socialist system in front of your kids.

If you wonder why our young people in the US find socialism so appealing and support the Marxist-Socialist Bernie Sanders, wonder no more. Marxism-Socialism has infiltrated our schools and especially our colleges. New socialists are graduated every year. They consider freedom and capitalism bad, while socialist serfdom is good.

10.11.   Freedom

Unlike Lenin, Trotsky, and Stalin, Hitler didn't have to kill millions of his people. Hitler lured the German people to accept National-Socialism with socialist promises. And the German people voted Hitler into power, and in exchange they relinquished their liberty, their freedom. Lenin, on the other hand, imposed his political system with the power of the gun.

Hitler said:

> The decisive question is who enlightens the people, who educates them? In those countries, it is actually capital that rules; that is, nothing more than a clique of a few hundred men who possess untold wealth and, as a consequence of the peculiar structure of their national life, are more or less independent and free. They say: "Here we have liberty." By this they mean, above all, an uncontrolled economy, and by an uncontrolled economy, the freedom not only to acquire capital but to make absolutely free use of it. That means freedom from national control or control by the people both in the acquisition of capital and its employment. [4: Berlin, Rheinmetall-Borsig Works – Speech of Decembern10, 1940]

Who needs this kind of capitalistic freedom? Your employment, your education, what you read in the papers, and the national decision-making is all in the hands of a few hundred capitalists. The National-Socialism state will take care of you in our name, as the decisions will be made for the good of all the community. You don't need that kind of useless freedom.

Allegedly, Lenin said:
> It is true that liberty is precious; so precious that it must be carefully rationed.
> No amount of political freedom will satisfy the hungry masses.

Just like Adolf Hitler, Vladimir Ilych Lenin was a mass murderer and an evil Communist-Socialist genius. Liberty and freedom can lead men astray. They must be kept, and nourished, on the "wholesome" diet of socialist serfdom, where they are told what to read, what to think, what to eat, where to work, how much education or medical assistance to get, and even how many kids to have. If you were born in freedom, do you understand it? If you don't have freedom, do you know it? Something to ponder, when freedom will be abolished in our country.

But what exactly is this liberty or freedom? According to Wikipedia:
> Liberty is the ability to do as one pleases. . ..
> Thus liberty entails the responsible use of freedom under the rule of law without depriving anyone else of their freedom. Freedom is more broad in that it represents a total lack of restraint or the unrestrained ability to fulfill one's desires.

Hmm! Per the above definition, everyone has liberty in any system of government—communism, socialism, nationalism, democracy, or fascism—as long as one exercises that freedom as allowed within that political system.

I remember when I was in high school and we were learning about the Communist-Socialist Romanian constitution, compliments of the Soviet Union, of course. We had all the liberty we needed and then some, more than any other country. The communist constitution guaranteed freedom of speech, providing that you speak for [communism-socialism], and did not speak against [communism-socialism]. You can put any words you consider undesirable between the brackets, and after you exhaust all things you cannot say, there will be limited vocabulary to use to express yourself for your daily needs. The constitution was very precise about what you could say and what you could not say. Political correctness at its best. This is what liberty and freedom are in any socialist totalitarian state.

10.12.   Population's Welfare

"Welfare" in this context implies "well-to-do," how well the people are doing economically, not the American "welfare" system.

The Great Depression hit in 1929, and in 1933 the NAZI-Socialist party was voted into power with the hope of bringing in a prosperous future. Germany had more than six million unemployed and, like most of the world, could not get out of the depression. What plans did the NAZI-Socialists have? Promises that they'd do better, by eliminating the inefficiency of the Weimar Democracy, profiteering, and exploitation of the people. They would provide land reform, and jobs.

According to Hitler:

> A concerned and all-embracing attack must be made on unemployment in order that the German working class may be saved from ruin.
> [4: Berlin: Proclamation to the German Nation – February 1, 1933]

But how do you create jobs? In a Communist-Socialist country, the economy is in the hands of the government. Therefore, the government is the *only employer*, and the government will put everyone to work, if you want it to or not. Wonderful, but why doesn't a democratic free economy do the same during a depression? The issue is money. A Communist-Socialist state owns the banks and treasury, and their currency is worthless, just printed paper good only within that country. Communist-Socialist countries were hungry for hard currency, as it is the only internationally accepted currency in the world. Even the Communist-Socialist countries had to trade among themselves in hard currency: dollars, not their national currency. The government can print more money and have enough to pay everyone, albeit with a lot lower buying power than before. The newly employed are put to work in any sector of the economy, from manufacturing, to agriculture, to sanitation, to transportation, and so on. There are no unemployed. There are no soup kitchens. If you don't work where you're assigned, you starve.

In a democracy, in a free economy, jobs are provided by the government in government organizations, such as departmental institutions and the military. The money for paying the government employees comes from taxes or from borrowing, in the form of bonds for large projects. The Weimar government started public construction works to put people to work. One of these was the Autobahn. Hitler took credit for finishing it. But those jobs were not enough to remediate the massive unemployment. What could the NAZI-Socialist do better than the previous government? The NAZI-Socialist government did not nationalize the industry, other than the railroad and banking, although they expropriated the wealth of the Jews. Even with that confiscated money, there were not enough funds to employ six million people.

Hitler had another game in mind: rearmament, building up the military forces and financing the defense contractors to manufacture tanks, trucks, guns, airplanes, and submarines. And that's how Hitler solved the unemployment of the Great Depression in Germany. Using all kinds of financial schemes, borrowing as much as the NAZI-Socialists could from banks and from the retirement plans of workers, Germany restarted its economy, but with little public disclosure of how much rearming was done. The Treaty of Versailles prohibited Germany from rearming, but Hitler did it in secret and solved the unemployment problem.

Hitler said:

> When I took power there were more than 6,000,000 unemployed and the farmers seemed doomed to decay. Today you must admit that I have fulfilled my promises. [4: Berlin, Reichstag–Speech of January 30, 1937]

NAZI Germany became the economic wonder of the world. Other countries sent emissaries to learn how they did it. Hitler said:

> My whole economic system has been built up on the concentration of work. We have solved

problems while, amazingly enough, the capitalist countries and their currencies have suffered bankruptcy. [4: Berlin, Rheinmetall-Borsig Works – Speech of December10, 1940]

One difference was that Germany had not a democracy, but a totalitarian socialist government. This government was free to do as it pleased without much deliberation or opposition. And as long as it worked, everyone was happy.

Building the military is an expense to the government that produces jobs but no other wealth after the products are delivered. Tanks cannot be used to harvest the fields. Hitler did not finance the armament industry to create jobs. The jobs were a byproduct, very much needed employment. The NAZI-Socialist government needed a strong military to invade the Soviet Union, a way for the military assets to produce wealth: conquer another country and acquire its wealth for the invader's socialist benefits.

To placate the labor activists for the loss of their power and to gratify the workers, institutions were created to provide people with vacations in government-built facilities and spas. This is socialism at its best. It is good to reward the workers with places for recreation—and for indoctrination as well. The truth was that in a socialist country the workers were paid so poorly that affording a vacation at one's own expense was impossible. Since the state takes care of you from cradle to grave, why not provide recreation and bring some happiness to the masses?

Through the initiatives of *Kraft durch Freude* (Strength through Joy) and *Schonheit der Arbeit* (Beauty of Work) the German workers felt that the NAZI-Socialist state was taking care of them.

All work and no play make a German worker dull and gray.

These programs were what provoked me to look into Hitler as a socialist.

From *Hitler* by Joachim C. Fest:

> They looked into the widely ramified system of social benefits: the improvement of labor conditions, the factory canteens and workers' housing, the newly established athletic fields, parks, kindergartens, the plant contests and professional competitions, the Strength-Through-Joy fleet of cruise ships and the people's vacation resorts. The model of a hotel for the masses, planned to extend for about 2½ miles on the island of Rugen, with its own special subway system to shuttle the tens of thousands of vacationers. [2: pg 509]

The above description of what Hitler and NAZI-Socialism did for the German people in those days is identical to what the Communism-Socialism government did in Romania. I can attest that in Romania the government provided factory canteens and workers' apartment housing, athletic fields, parks, kindergartens, plant contests and athletic competitions, and the peoples' vacation resorts in the mountains and along the Black Sea. If you think that this description of Romanian social improvements is identical to what Joachim Fest said about NAZI-Germany above, it is identical not in words but in deeds. Adolf Hitler and his party were first-class socialists. The USSR would have been proud.

The hotels on the Black Sea shores of Mamaia, Constanta, in Romania and the complex of Prora at Rugen in Germany were both constructed by the Socialist state for the benefit of the people.

Although these resorts might look like Miami beach, they were built by the government for the workers' enjoyment, not by entrepreneurs for the hotel industry and leisure.

You may wonder what's so bad about the state providing for people's recreational needs. Nothing. I'm not suggesting that these initiatives were bad. They were actually good if the people were so destitute and poorly paid that they could not afford vacations on their own. However, expect vacations resembling summer camps, mass transportation, common housing, canteen meals, and group exercises to keep everyone busy. And also expect banners with slogans praising socialism and political speeches served up day and night.

Everyone knows the VW Beatle. The old Beatle was the NAZI's car. It was Hitler who initiated the creation of an affordable car for the Germans. Unlike Henry Ford, who was motivated to expand the car market with an affordable Model T, the government in a socialist state accomplishes that task. Considering that Germany had an Autobahn but very few cars on it and that in America the roads were full of cars, Hitler had to show how well the people under socialism were doing. And so the VW Beatle was created, a car in every German's garage.

It cost only 750 marks, and the buyer would have to save five marks a week until he had the money to buy it. Unfortunately, WWII started, and production switched to war materiel. The car buyers' savings were also used for the war effort. Hardly any citizen acquired or drove a VW.

Under Communism-Socialism, East Germany built a people's car as well, the "famous" Trabant, which sounded like a sewing machine when it started. Communist-Socialist Romania had to have a car of its own too. A buyer was required to have the entire purchase amount in cash. Then the order was placed. Six months later, the car was delivered to the dealer. By the way, in the socialist spirit, even the colors of the cars were proportionally produced. The population could not have more of one color than another on the roads. Choice was not part of socialist life; you get what you get.

I remember from my youth in Romania: After many years of saving, one of my uncles bought a Dacia, the Romanian car. The new cars were delivered to the dealer in lots and in various colors. If he wanted a red car, he hoped it was in the delivered lot and that he was first to claim it. Otherwise, he got whatever color was left: beige or white.

10.13.   Central Planning

Central Planning of the economy is the mainstay of the Socialist state. It is a necessity, considering that the economy doesn't operate by free-market rules but by socialist directives.

Hitler said:

> The National Government intends to solve the problem of the reorganization of trade and commerce with two four-year plans. [4]

150

Communism-Socialism operates in five-year planning cycles, and the goals are always achieved or exceeded on paper, while the people's welfare does not improve. For NAZI-Socialist Germany, central planning was essential for rearming the military forces. It was also part of the command-and-control aspect of the socialist system. Nothing is allowed to happen haphazardly.

The German economy was in private hands, but the central planning was under Hermann Goering. Goering told the industrialists what to produce for how much and how many units. The War Economy, *Wehrwirtschaft*, was how the NAZI German economy operated, as described by Joachim Fest:

> A Four-Year Plan on the Soviet Russian model was to supply the sinews for the "Lebensraum" policy. Herman Goring was put in charge. He promptly proceeded to bully the businessmen into carrying out the plans for autarchy and rearmament without regard to the costs or the economic consequences. At the ministerial session devoted to Hitler's memorandum, Goring insisted that the country must act "as if we were in the stage of imminent peril of war."
> A few months later, he told a meeting of big businessmen that producing economically no longer mattered; What counted was simply to produce at all. [2: pg 537]

Central Planning does not follow free-market rules. It follows state rules. In the case of Germany, the goal was armament for war with the USSR.

In the Communist-Socialist countries, the decisions were made by bureaucrats, as decided by the Central Committee and directed by the ministries. The decisions were made based on whatever social, political, or "we are the greatest" need there was with little concern for the socioeconomic results, or demand and supply rules.

Chapter 11. The Communist Manifesto's Ten Rules

Let's examine how Nazi-Socialism applied each of the ten rules of the Communist Manifesto.

Rule 1
Abolition of property in land and application of all rents of land to public purposes.

- ☭ The most important reason that Hitler did not nationalize the economy was his desire to expand east as soon as possible. He didn't want the delays and work slowdowns of a nationalized economy. The industrialists would have fought him and delayed his war against the Soviet Union if nationalization had happened.

- ☭ Nazi-Socialists did not abolish private property. This is one of the main deviations from Marxism-Socialism. Confiscation of private property causes major economic disruptions in a country. Even the Bolsheviks did not confiscate all property all at once, especially land from smaller farmers, until Stalin was in charge. Although the economy was in private hands in Germany, the capitalists did what the NAZI party leadership told them to do. Besides he was going to confiscate another country's property, not Germany's.

- ☭ Hitler either realized that you don't kill the goose that lays the golden eggs or he looked at the Soviet

Union and saw the depressed state of its nationalized economy. Bad example not to follow.

☭ Although this Marxist rule is intended to eliminate exploitation and enrichment at the expense of another fellow man, the number one reason that Marxist-Socialists follow this rule is the elimination of any opposition. People with money can overthrow a government. In a Communist-Socialist state, the wealth and money are controlled and are the property of the state.

☭ Communist China, under Deng Xiaoping, relaxed the monopoly on the economy, allowing private property and profit. This was the salvation of Communist China. By maintaining the oligarchy and the party rule and allowing private enterprise—capitalism—and personal profit, China has become a National-Socialist country.

☭ Why was Hitler not afraid of the industrialists? His evil mind understood better than the Marxists-Socialists how economic and political control works. Strasser asked Hitler if, when the NAZI-Socialists took power, would the means of production be nationalized. Hitler responded:

> Do you think I am so mad as to destroy the economy? The State would intervene only if the employers were not acting in the interests of the nation. [2]

Joachim Fest wrote:

> The businessmen, contrary to the theory that capitalist interests were a dominant force in the Third Reich, proved willing tools who "had no more influence upon the political decisions, than their day laborers." Should they fail to meet the demands set

> for them, "it is not Germany that would be
> ruined, but at most a few managers," Hitler
> has hinted as early as the autumn of 1936
> in a memorandum concerning his
> economic program. [2: pg 537]

Marxism-Socialism ruins the economy of any country it gets hold of. Hitler had the foresight to maintain the efficiency of the German economy by not nationalizing it and by letting the industrialist experts run it. And if the industrialists did not comply with his orders, the managers would suffer the consequences. He had the police power and the concentration camps to ensure compliance.

☭ Just because Hitler did not nationalize the entire economy, he was not about to leave every institution independent. As he said:

> All those institutions which are the
> strongholds of the energy and vitality of
> our nation will be taken under the special
> care of the Government. I deprive the
> German railways and the Reichsbank of
> their former character and place them both
> without reservation under the sovereignty
> of the Government. [4: Berlin: Proclamation to the
> German Nation – February 1, 1933]

☭ Land ownership came with conditions. The state decides who owns land and can intervene in case the land or property is not used in the national (peoples') interest. From *The Program of the Party of Hitler*:

> To the right to hold property, however, is
> attached the obligation to use it in the
> national interest. [6]

In other words, the peasants were mere custodians of the land and had to produce or loose the right to the land. This could also be called "land serfdom." A similar situation to that is in China today.

After the October Revolution in the Soviet Union, the peasants helped themselves to the land and kept it for ten years until Stalin moved against them to collectivize agriculture.

Rule 2
A heavy progressive or graduated income tax.

☭ The NAZI-Socialist strategy was not to tax the capitalists into poverty. Hitler wanted them to prosper and to comply with his rearmament mandates. The taxation plan was as follows:

> Where enterprises continued in private hands, the personnel were to be entitled to a share of ten percent of the profits, the national government thirty percent, the country to six and the local community to five percent. [2]

The workers would be entitled to 10 percent of the profits. How socialist is this? Everyone was entitled to a piece of the pie. This tax plan may not have been implemented because the war began.

What did the Soviet worker receive? Nothing. There were no profits since the state owned everything.

Rule 3
Abolition of all rights of inheritance.

☭ Marxism wants to abolish all inheritances, so there will be no wealthy people or people with enough wealth not needing to work. Hitler intended to abolish the inheritance of land. Since all land was the property of the state, the children were not entitled to it unless they continued working it as their parents had.

Rule 4
Confiscation of the property of all emigrants and rebels.

☭ Considering how many Jews and non-Jews fled Germany because of NAZI-Socialism, this was applied in full by Hitler.

Rule 5
Centralization of credit in the hands of the State, by means of a national bank with State capital and an exclusive monopoly.

☭ Any totalitarian socialist state has complete control of money, and so did Hitler. This is contrary to a democratic state, as in the United States with the Federal Reserve. The German economy had to improve, and there wouldn't be any interference by an independent central bank in any of Hitler's borrowing for the domestic and military buildup.

Rule 6
Centralization of the means of communication and transport in the hands of the State.

☭ The state owns all means of *communication*, like the post office, the telephone, the telegraph, and radio. All transportation, like ships, trains, busses, trucks, and perhaps even cars, will be state property. Controlling the means of communication and transport are essential in a totalitarian state. It controls or restricts the dissemination of information and the movement of people.

Accordingly, Hitler said:

> These capitalists create their own press and then speak of "freedom of the press." In reality, every one of the newspapers has a master, and in every case the master is the capitalist, the owner. This master, not the editor, is the one who directs the policy of the paper. . .. This press, which is the absolutely submissive and characterless slave of the owners, molds public opinion.
> [4: Berlin, Rheinmetall-Borsig Works – Speech December 10, 1940]

All the institutions that dealt with communication or dissemination of information were under the control of the Minister of Propaganda, Joseph Goebbels. The German people read, saw, and heard only what the NAZI-Socialist party allowed.

In North Korea, radio and TV access only government stations. In China, even the internet is censored or controlled by the Communist party with the full cooperation of Google. In the United States, on the other hand, we are controlled by the leftist mainstream media, and Facebook, Twitter, and Google.

ॐ The major means of transportation in Germany at the time were the railways, which in most cases in Europe were government monopolies.

Rule 7
Extension of factories and instruments of production owned by the State; the bringing into cultivation of wastelands and the improvement of soil generally in accordance with a common plan.

ॐ Although the industry was not owned by the state, the NAZI-Socialist German economy performed under a centralized planning system just like the Soviet Union. The NAZI-Socialist State controlled even the agricultural trades, as the *The Program of the Party of Hitler* stated:

> The settlement of prices for agriculture produce must be freed from market speculation, and a stop must be put to exploitation of the agricultural interest by large middlemen. [6: pg 16]

Besides, since all land was regulated by the NAZI-Socialist state, and committed to be used productively, *cultivation of wastelands* was a given.

159

Rule 8
Equal liability of all to labor. Establishment of industrial armies, especially for agriculture.

☭ How close is what Hitler said to rule eight from *The Communist Manifesto*? The two are nearly identical. Hitler said in one of his speeches:

> Compulsory labor-service and the back-to-the-land policy are two of the basic principles of this program. [4: Berlin: Proclamation to the German Nation – February 1, 1933]

☭ Everyone must work to partake in the society's benefits. Hitler said:

> What we want is not a state of drones but a State which gives to everyone that to which on the basis of his own activity he has the right. He who refuses to do honest work shall not be a citizen of the State. [4]

In Communist-Socialist countries like Romania, everyone had to work, unless your parents supported you. There was no welfare or unemployment pay unless one was physically handicapped. Hitler's words reflect the same socialist attitude toward the workers that was held in Communist-Socialist Romania under the motto: "We are building our socialist country."

Rule 9
Combination of agriculture with manufacturing industries; gradual abolition of the distinction of town and country by a more equable distribution of the population over the country.

- ☭ Hitler couldn't have been bothered with social engineering or population redistribution before the war. However, he applied this rule to slave labor, moving people from their native lands to work on war projects.
- ☭ Later on, after concluding the war, victorious Hitler had ambitious plans for the newly conquered lands and their populations, falling in line with Rule 9.

Rule 10
Free education of all children in public schools. Abolition of children's factory labor in its present form. Combination of education with industrial production, etc., etc.

- ☭ In one of his speeches Hitler said:

  As you know we have countless schools, national political educational establishments, Adolf Hitler schools, and so on. To these schools we send gifted children of the broad masses, children of working men, of farmers, sons whose parents could never have afforded a higher education for their children. [4: Berlin,

Dumitru Sandru

Rheinmetall-Borsig Works – Speech of Decembern10, 1940]

Controlling the schools is essential in keeping the people on the same page, sort of speaking. Not to ignore that schooling also serves as the indoctrination institution for following and obeying the system.

Who determines the agenda and curriculum for our schools? The United States Government; hardly. The schools have long ago been infiltrated by the neo-Marxist-Leninist advocates, and the same with the school unions. They are deciding how to shape the future of our country, not the government or the people of this country.

Chapter 12. NAZI-Socialism's Twenty-five Point Political Program

Marxist-Socialism has *The Communist Manifesto* with its ten rules to guide them into making everyone equally poor. NAZI-Socialism had its "NSDAP Twenty-five Points Political Program" as the guiding principles for what NAZI-Socialism stood for and what it intended to accomplish. The following abbreviated list is extracted from Wikipedia. I'm noting which point is nationalistic or socialistic or both.

 Point 1

We want all Germans to live in a "Germany."

Nationalistic: Many Germans lived outside Germany, in Austria, Sudetenland, Poland. This point dictates that all lands adjacent to Germany with German populations be integrated into the Third Reich.

 Point 2

We want Germany to be treated the same as other nations, and we want the peace treaties of Versailles to be cancelled.

Nationalistic: Germany was to be restored to the situation prior to 1914.

 Point 3

We want land and territory (colonies) to feed our people and to settle our surplus population.

Socialistic: This is *Lebensraum*, "room to grow," and justification for conquering other nations. Hitler wished:

> If I had the Ural Mountains with their incalculable store of treasures in raw materials, Siberia with its vast forests, and the Ukraine with its tremendous wheat fields, Germany and the National Socialist leadership, would swim in plenty! [4: Nuremberg Speech September 14, 1936]

 Point 4

Only Germans may be citizens of Germany. Only those of the German races may be members of the nation, their religion does not matter. No Jew may be a citizen.

Nationalistic/racist: The Jews, even if citizens, were excluded from being Germans.

 Point 5

Non-citizens may live in Germany, but there will be special laws for foreigners living in Germany.

Nationalistic: Anti-foreign workers.

Point 6

Only citizens can vote for parliament and councils, or vote on laws. Everyone who works for the German government, a state government or even a small village must be a citizen of Germany. We will stop giving people jobs because of the political party they are in. Only the best people should get a job.

Nationalistic and socialistic: Only ethnic Germans are citizens, and only they can vote. The last democratic vote was in 1933. After that year, plebiscites were the only votes allowed. The Reichstag existed only in name.

 Point 7

Every citizen has a job. We think that the government's first job is to make sure every citizen has a job and enough to eat. If the government cannot do this, people who are not citizens should be made to leave Germany.

Socialistic and nationalistic: The responsibility to provide belongs to the government, and it has the responsibility to deport foreigners if the economy can sustain only Germans.

Hitler and the National-Socialist party achieved full employment by 1935, only two years after taking power.

Point 8

No one who is not of a German race should be allowed to live in Germany. We want anyone who is not of a German race who started living in Germany after 2 August 1914 to leave the country.

Nationalistic: Jews or other nationalities must leave Germany. This would liberate resources for the Germans.

 Point 9

All citizens shall have equal rights and duties.

Socialistic: Similar to #8 in the Communist Manifesto.

 Point 10

Every citizen should have a job. Their work should not be selfish, but help everyone.

Socialistic: Similar to #8 in the Communist Manifesto.

Most people want a job to survive, and Hitler eliminated most unemployment by re-arming the country.

 Point 11

The abolition of incomes unearned by work. The breaking of the slavery of interest.

Socialistic: Similar to #1 in the Communist Manifesto.

Point 12

Confiscate war profits. So many people die or lose their property in a war, it is wrong for other people to make money from the war. Anyone who made money from the war should have all that money taken away.

Socialistic: Confiscation of war *profits*. Similar to #1 in Communist Manifesto.

 Point 13

We want all very big corporations to be owned by the government.

Socialistic: Similar to #1 in the Communist Manifesto. It was not implemented because of the war.

 Point 14

Big industrial companies should share their profits with the workers.

Socialistic: Similar to #2 in the Communist Manifesto.

 Point 15

We want old age pensions to be increased.

Socialistic: Old-age welfare/Social Security. The elderly have always been an easy target to capture votes for the party by giving them better pensions.

Point 16

We want a healthy middle class:
- *to create a healthy middle class*
- *to split up big department stores, and let small traders rent space inside them*
- *to make State and town governments try to buy from small traders.*

Socialistic: Similar to #2 in the Communist Manifesto.

 Point 17

We want to change the way land is owned. We also want:
- *a law to take over land if the country needs it, without the government having to pay for   it.*
- *to abolish ground rent, and*
- *to prohibit land speculation (buying land just to sell to someone else for more money).*

Socialistic: Land redistribution. Similar to #1 in the Communist Manifesto.

In *The Program of the Party of Hitler* the clarification about this point is as follows:

> German land may not become an object of financial speculation, nor may it provide an unearned income for its owner. It may only be acquired by him who is prepared to cultivate it himself.
>
> Only the members of the German nation may possess land.
>
> To the right to hold property, however, is attached the obligation to use it in the national interest. [6: pg 14]

168

Point 18

Crimes against the common interest must be punished with death.

Nationalistic and Socialistic: Crimes against the State, including political dissent, are always punishable by death. Many factory directors in Communist-Socialist Romania were executed when major factory accidents happened. They were negligent; they caused damage to the economy. Off with their heads!

 Point 19

We want the Roman law system changed for the German common law system.

Socialistic and Nationalistic: Adopt German Common Law, which viewed crimes as being against individuals, unlike that of France's Roman Law, which viewed crimes being against the state.

 Point 20

We want to change the system of schools and education, so that every hard-working German can have the chance of higher education.

- *What is taught should concentrate on practical things.*
- *Schools should teach civic affairs so that children can become good citizens.*

- *If poor parents cannot afford to pay, the government should pay for education.*
Socialistic: Similar to #10 in the Communist Manifesto.

 Point 21

The State must protect health standards by
- *protecting mothers and infants*
- *stopping children from working*
- *making a law for compulsory gymnastics and sports, and*
- *supporting sports clubs for young men.*
Socialistic: Similar to #10 in the Communist Manifesto.

 Point 22

We want to get rid of the old army and replace it with a people's army that would look after the ordinary people, not just the rich officer class
Socialistic: Elimination of social classes.

Point 23

We want the law to stop politicians from being anti-German, and newspapers from writing about them. To make a German national press we demand:

• *that all editors of and writers in the German language newspapers are members of the nation (of a German race);*

• *Foreign newspapers need permission from the government. They must not be printed in the German language; any non-German who does own or control a newspaper will be made to leave Germany, and the newspaper closed down,*

• *Non-Germans cannot own or control German newspapers.*

• *Newspapers which criticize the country or the government are not allowed.*

• *Art and books which support foreign ideas should be banned.*

Socialistic and Nationalistic: Elimination of freedom of speech. Similar to #6 in Communist Manifesto.

 Point 24

We want to allow all religions in the State, unless they offend the moral feelings of the German race. The NSDAP is Christian but does not belong to any denomination. The NSDAP will fight the Jewish self-interest spirit and believes that our nation will be strongest only if everyone puts the common interest before self-interest.

Socialistic and Nationalistic: Although this sounds like freedom of religion, only the religions that benefit the state interests would be allowed.

 Point 25

We will create a strong central government.
- *create a strong central government for the Reich;*
- *give Parliament control over the entire government and its organizations;*
- *form groups based on class and job to carry out the laws in the various German states.*

Socialistic: Although it sounds like democracy, it is not. It proposes a strong central government.

In case you still wonder why the party's name was National-Socialist, the above points should make it clear. The Nationalistic aspect is no different than all communist-Socialist countries in Europe; exception is the anti-Jew sentiment.

Karl Marx couldn't have written better socialist points, but they were written by Adolf Hitler and the National Socialist party. Socialism always intends well, and its directives can be accomplished only through a centralized totalitarian form of government. Delivering what it promises has never happened or will ever happen.

Chapter 13. The Holocaust

Socialism exterminates the people who oppose it, those it considers undesirable and unredeemable. This trait is applicable to both National-Socialism and Communist-Socialism.

One of the most heinous acts of socialism was the extermination of people by the NAZI-Socialists because of their race: almost six million Jews killed. The Holocaust happened between 1941 and 1945. What's even worse is that the Jews were productive members of the German society. Hitler used hatred of Jews as a propaganda tool at first. Then when the United States entered World War II, he accused the Jews of provoking that war, justifying the industrial extermination of the Jews.

Note: Fascist Franco's Spain did not engage in killing the Jews. As a matter of fact, hundreds of thousands of Jews, running away from Germany and France, found refuge in Spain. This is not intended to make fascism seem more humane but to emphasize that Socialism was responsible for the Holocaust.

After the Anschluss of Austria and the conquering of Poland, many Jews were held in ghettos until the *Final Solution* to exterminate them was decided upon, after which they were taken to the extermination camps. The Jews in the ghettos self-administered their communities and even decided who to send on the next train to the death camps. Eventually, the last Jews remaining, including their leaders, were packed up and sent to their demise as well.

After the invasion of the USSR in 1941, Hitler was determined to exterminate all Jews in all the conquered territories. But the NAZIs were not the only Jew killers. The Latvians and Ukrainians did their part by shooting Jews, by the tens of thousands, on the edges of mass graves so they could bury them quickly and eliminate any trace of their homicide. Many other countries, like Romania, Hungary, Bulgaria, and others, participated in the killing of Jews or in deporting them to the death camps in Poland.

Early on, Jews were shot. But shooting was too slow, so the NAZI-Socialists used vans in the 1940s, piping exhaust gases into the vans to asphyxiate the passengers, but that was inefficient as well. Many Jews were killed over a period of time from exhaustion and famine in the slave labor camps or in ghettos. Toward the end of the war, the Jews were sent directly to the extermination camps to be killed in Dachau, Treblinka, Auschwitz-Birkenau, and many others.

The NAZI-Socialists created an industrial murdering machine, gathering the Jews, transporting them, killing them, and then disposing of their bodies by incineration. The Jews were transported by train from far away territories to the concentration camps in Poland. They were taken off the train and separated into those who could work and those who would die immediately. The victims were taken to the "showers," where they were gassed with Zyklon-B, Hydrogen Cyanide. They died within twenty minutes, and the *Sonderkommando*, workers, made up mostly of Jews, removed the bodies and then removed gold fillings, jewelry, and eyeglasses. They cut the women's hair and then took the bodies to the crematorium where they were burned. Eventually, the *Sonderkommando* were gassed as well so that there would be no witnesses to the horror. Why did some Jews work for the extermination camps and process their brethren's corpses? To live a few more months. They knew they too would be killed in the gas chambers. Imagine the twisted reality they lived in their final days.

Toward the end of the war, the victims—men, women, and children—were no longer sorted but, upon arrival at the camps, sent directly to the gas chambers to be killed. This horror ended when the Russians were too close to the camps. Most of the camps were blown apart to hide the horror committed there. The following are pictures I took at Auschwitz-Birkenau:

The Gates of Hell

The Barracks

The Furnace

What is little known is that Stalin, in the Soviet Union, used "gas vans" from 1936–38 to execute those condemned to death. There were so many sentenced to death during those years that on the way to the execution site at Butovo the condemned were killed by asphyxiation in specially modified vans, exhausting the engine gasses into the van, very similar to what the NAZI-Socialists would do later. Upon arrival at Butovo, the dead were taken to mass graves without wasting bullets, eliminating the messy business of shooting the condemned prisoners one-by-one in the back of the head or on the firing line.

Who invented the gas vans? The Soviet-Socialists used them first in 1936, and the NAZI-Socialists used them in 1940. What's even more interesting is where the concentration camps, for forced labor or extermination, came from. According to *The Black Book of Communism*:

> The Reich Security Head Office issued to the commandants a full collection of reports concerning the Russian concentration camps. These described in great detail the condition in, and organization of, the Russian camps, as supplied by former prisoners who had managed to escape. Great emphasis was placed on the fact that the Russians, by their massive employment of forced labor, had destroyed whole peoples. [9: pg 15]

Therefore, contrary to what has been said, the Communist-Socialist USSR originated the use of concentration camps for slave labor and extermination. The NAZIs emulated them for the same purpose, slavery and forced labor or extermination.

From the *The Black Book of Communism* on the USSR and Chinese concentration camps and the prisoners there:

> The concentration-camp system was turned into a "reeducation system" and the tyrants became "educators" who transformed the people of the old society into "new people." The zeks, a term used for Soviet concentration-camp prisoners, were forcibly "invited" to place their trust in the system that enslaved them. In China the concentration-camp prisoner is called a "student" and he is required to study the correct thoughts of the Party and to reform his own faulty thinking. [9: pg 19]

All these "students" in Chinese camps are used as slave labor making products for exporting to the US, or as organ donors when the "students" are sentenced to death.

Sad, but true:

Socialism of any persuasion will kill with impunity.

Chapter 14. The Socialist Promise Crumbles

The miracle of full employment happened under NAZI-Socialism. There were no more soup lines and beggars in the streets. Means of cheap entrainment and recreation were made available. But prospering was another thing, which was diligently fogged up by the continuous NAZI-Socialist propaganda, by working for the betterment of the nation, of the German people.

As stated in The Program of the Party of Hitler:

> A general lowering of prices, at the same time maintaining wages at the present level, would be the better and more practical way to fulfil the demand for sharing out the profits of the whole of our national production . . . the national Socialist State will solve the problem in a far more comprehensive manner than is conceived today by brains with a Marxist and capitalistic tendency. The present demand for profit-sharing springs either from a desire for profits (essentially capitalistic) or from envy (essentially Marxist). [6]

This is a most interesting statement, justifying the reason that National Socialism was superior to Marxist Socialism or capitalism. The redistribution of wealth did not come from profit sharing but from keeping the wages at a level where the prices for goods were low as well. Although NAZI-Socialism proposed a ten percent share in profits originally, that never happened. Neither did land reform promises ever happen. The NAZI Socialists hoped for new land in the conquered territories.

Inevitably, everywhere, all the socialist promises come to an end after they exhaust other people's wealth. In the case of NAZI-Socialist Germany, most of the other people's money, the money taken from the Jews or from workers' pension funds, was used for rearmament and consequently create jobs. Germany's industrial power produced weapons, not for export but for future use in war. Since the industrial production for exports diminished, so did the nation's foreign-exchange reserves, making it harder for Germany to buy food from abroad.

Shortages began prior to the start of the war, and with shortages, hoarding began, making matters even worse during those years. NAZI-Socialist propaganda began justifying the shortages and warning against hoarding.

In one of his speeches, Hitler said:

> That is why in order to ensure equal distribution, we have had to impose certain restrictions from the very start.
>
> The question was asked: "Will meat be rationed?" That was the first sounding of a warning. In other words: "If you are a capitalist, cover your requirements, buy yourself a refrigerator and hoard up a few sides of bacon."
> [4: Berlin, Rheinmetall-Borsig Works – Speech of December n 10, 1940]

Shortages increased as the war began, but the German people had other things on their minds besides scarcities as the France and Great Britain declared war on Germany. The German people were not keen on going to war, as the last war was only twenty-one years before.

Hitler Was a Socialists

Shortages are a mainstay of Socialism. Not because the country lacks resources, but because the country is managed by incompetent bureaucrats without knowledge of free market economy. I grew up with shortages, having to wait in long lines with my parents to buy the necessities of life. And toilet paper was seldom available. As socialism matures, it gets worse as it did in Romania after I left in 1971. As an example, the largest wattage light bulb available was 40 Watt. That was because of lack of producing electricity efficiently. By lowering the electrical consumption in the country, there was a surplus, and that excess electricity was sold to neighboring countries for hard currency.

Look today at Communist-Socialist Cuba. It rations food after sixty plus years of socialism? While the Soviet Union and the other Communist-Socialist countries were in power, they supported Cuba, as an important outpost near the USA. The socialist benefactors collapsed, and the socialist life showed its dark colors in Cuba. Along came Chavez in Venezuela, and Cuba gets to buy oil at subsidized prices and resell it for a profit, and socialist life improves, always with other people's money. Under Maduro, Socialist Venezuela's economy deteriorated so badly that it could not support Cuba with cheap oil any longer. And Cuba returns to food rationing. All this happens because Marxism-Socialism does not allow freedom and profit. If they would, there will be plenty in Cuba.

In spite of the improving economy and employment, shortages began to occur in NAZI-Germany before the war, but after the victory over France, which now had to pay Germany war damages, life improved slightly. Even though Germany just conquered Western Europe, the German economy was not producing any more armament than before, in other words the economy was not producing on a foot of war. As the war continued and millions of young men were called to fight in the war and the economy was geared for war only, the welfare of the people began declining, reaching starvation levels as the war ended.

Chapter 15. War World II

"The German Nation wishes to live in peace with the rest of the world," [4] said Hitler in another of his speeches. And probably he meant it as long as he was going to achieve his goals of fulfilling the socialist promises by conquering other lands. Nationalism-Socialism and Communism-Socialism intend well at first—economic equality for all. But they go about it two different ways:

☭ The Marxist-Socialist strategy for equalizing wealth is achieved by cannibalizing the nation's assets and "redistributing" them, elimination of personal freedom and elimination of profit. Those are the reasons that no socialist economy has ever succeeded, or will ever succeed. But before the Socialist state runs out of other people's money and collapses, it will export its philosophy to other countries and conquer them politically or militarily. The Soviet Union acquired new lands in Central-Eastern Europe after the war. Before the war, Stalin had his eyes on Germany and did get part of it after the war. Why did the Soviet Union invade Afghanistan? What was Cuba doing in Angola or by supporting Nicaraguan Sandinistas and Chavez/Maduro Venezuela? Expanding its markets and acquiring more wealth to compensate for the Marxist-Socialist failures.

> The National-Socialist strategy for equalizing wealth was not to take from the nation's rich and give to the nation's poor, making everyone equally poor, but to acquire assets through conquering other nations and making the people of those nations poor. The war with the Soviet Union was inevitable. The premise of National-Socialism was to obtain new land and resources to satisfy the German people. Room to grow, *Lebensraum*.

The World War II starting in Western Europe was an accident, but the war in Eastern Europe was planned. It was part of Hitler's strategy. *Lebensraum*—room to grow—was what Hitler called the invasion of other nations for the benefit of his NAZI-Socialist nation. He even mentioned this plan in *Mein Kampf*, spelling out clearly his intention to expand east into Russia.

According to Joachim C. Fest:

> He realized that Europe could be dominated by a continental power that controlled western Russia, drew upon the reserves of Asia, and simultaneously presented itself as the advocate of the colonial nations by linking political revolution with slogans of social liberation. He also knew that he had gone to war with Soviet Union over the question of who would assume this part. [2]

After the end of World War I, the British Empire and France, as the winners, were "the power" in Europe. What emerged subsequently was a destroyed Germany that rose from its ashes and the Soviet Union with a new expansionary political system. Stalin wished to get his claws into Germany and enlarge his Communist empire, making use of German industries and the German people's work ethic and discipline. The Prime-Minister of Great Britain Neville Chamberlain saw the dilemma: a German-Soviet Union would become the largest power in the world, whoever conquered whom. That's why British politicians did not buy Hitler's proposal for Germany to destroy communism and keep Western Europe safe from Marxism. Churchill, as the guardian of the British Empire, and the United States had to choose which socialist country to fight. They feared German National-Socialism and Hitler more than they feared Soviet Communism-Socialism and Stalin, and rightly so. Although, the Soviet Union became a superpower *after* the war, time proved that it was a weak socialist power. Meanwhile, hundreds of millions of people suffered and died under the tyranny of the Communist-Socialist regimes.

World War II could have been avoided if Hitler hadn't overplayed his hand. Great Britain and France worried about the Anschluss, the joining of Austria with NAZI-Germany, but couldn't prevent it. It happened without a shot being fired and with most Austrians euphorically accepting their inclusion in the Third Reich. Hitler was on a roll, so to speak, in the acquisition of new land.

Point 1 of NAZI-Socialism's Twenty-five Points of the NAZI Political Program stated that *We want all Germans to live in a "Germany."* Hitler's ambition was to integrate all foreign lands neighboring Germany and with German populations into the Third Reich. Austria was the first step. The Sudetenland in Czechoslovakia was another such territory. But Czechoslovakia had a friendship/alliance with France, including an agreement that France would come to the Czech's aid in case of war. Hitler didn't think that France would raise a finger, and he was right. The British Prime Minister, Neville Chamberlain, wanted to maintain peace in Europe at all costs. Although France and Great Britain were the winners of World War I, they were weary and hesitant to wage a new war. It was just twenty years since that war had ended with millions of casualties and the destruction of wealth.

Therefore, Chamberlain intervened as a negotiator to appease Hitler and prevent Germany from invading Czechoslovakia. Without the involvement of the Czechoslovak government, Great Britain and France agreed at a meeting in Munich to let Germany annex Sudetenland if Hitler would promise that he had no more territorial claims against any other nation in Europe. Hitler signed the agreement, and Chamberlain flew back to England, waving the agreement from the door of his aircraft, promising that there will be "peace in our time." The German army occupied Sudetenland on October 1, 1938. But Hitler was greedy and wanted the whole country. The rest of Czechoslovakia was occupied in March 1939.

Chamberlain may have been a peace lover, but he was not a fool. It was obvious that Hitler had played him, and he was not going to allow that to happen again. Soon Hitler began making noises about Poland. To prevent another land acquisition by Germany, Great Britain and France offered Poland a protection treaty if invaded by Germany.

In 1918, per the Treaty of Versailles, Poland became independent, and eastern Prussia was separated from the rest of Germany to give Poland access to the sea. For Hitler to attack the Soviet Union, he needed a common border with that country, and Poland was in the way.

Besides Germany, the Soviet Union had an eye on Poland as well, perhaps wanting a common border with Germany for similar territorial expansion toward the west. The Soviet Union and Germany, under the Molotov–Ribbentrop Pact, agreed to divide Poland on August 23, 1939. Hitler did not believe that France and Great Britain would go to war to protect Poland, a land on the other side of Germany with no strategic value to them.

NAZI-Germany invaded Poland on Friday, September 1, 1939. As promised, France and Great Britain declared war on Germany on Monday, September 3, 1939. The Soviet Union invaded Poland on September 17, 1939, acquiring the other half of Poland. Subsequently, the Soviet Union invaded the Baltic States and portions of Romania.

It was not a World War II yet, just a war in Europe. And it was France and Great Britain who theoretically started it, although Germany provoked it by crossing the line. Of course, the whole British Empire and Commonwealth—Canada, Australia, New Zealand, and South Africa—along with France's territories, declared war on Germany as well, but without any fighting. In Western Europe there wasn't any military activity, other than the futile attempt by France to invade Germany in the Saar region.

To protect itself from Great Britain's Navy, Germany occupied Denmark and Norway in April 1940. On May 10, 1940, Germany attacked France by invading first the Netherlands, Belgium, and Luxemburg. And then, slogging through the Arden Forest, they encircled the allied armies, pushing them to Dunkirk where they escaped to Great Britain. France capitulated and signed an armistice with Germany on June 22, 1940. NAZI Germany had conquered most of Western Europe in six weeks.

Dumitru Sandru

But the war had just begun.

In a speech in 1944, Hitler admitted that the war was:
> ... a pre-financing of the future achievements, the future work, the future raw materials, the future nutritional base. [2: pg 614]

He didn't have to admit that he had already written in *Mein Kampf* in 1924 about *Lebensraum* and the expansion into the Soviet Union. In other speeches, he showed his antagonism toward Bolshevism and what he could do with their land:

> Bolshevism turns flourishing countryside into sinister wastes of ruins; National Socialism transforms a Reich of destruction and misery to a healthy State and a flourishing economic life.

> Russia planned a world revolution and German workmen would be used but as a cannon-fodder for bolshevist imperialism. But we National Socialists do not wish that our military resources should be employed to impose by force on other peoples what those peoples themselves do not want.

> Bolshevism has attacked the foundation of our whole human order, alike in State and society, the foundations of our conception of civilization, of our faith and our morals: all alike are at stake.

> These are only some of the grounds for the antagonism which separate us from communism. . .. Here are really two worlds which do but grow further apart from each other and can never unite. [4: Nuremberg Speech September 14, 1936]

To fulfill his Socialist dreams for NAZI Germany, on June 22, 1941, Hitler's Wehrmacht attacked the USSR and advanced to Leningrad, and near Moscow. They had conquered Stalingrad by December 1942. At these locations, NAZI-Socialist Germany was finally stopped.

The United States, through the Lend-Lease program, provided the Soviet Union with massive war materiel, technology, and weapons assistance that gave the Soviet Union the ability to start a counteroffensive. According to Wikipedia, the Soviet Union received from the United States 1,911 locomotives and 11,225 railcars, hundreds of thousands of trucks, 7,000 tanks, and 18,200 aircraft. Shipments of telephone cable, aluminum, canned rations, clothing, weapons, and ammunition, not to mention technological know-how, poured in. As a consequence, the Soviet Union's entire economy soared into the technological age. The Soviets copied all that technology and manufactured it as Russian later on.

Until the 1960s, in the streets of Romania, I saw trucks based on the Dodge three-quarter ton and Studebaker two-and-a-half ton models, painted in the same drab olive color as the war trucks. The Soviet bomber Tu-4 was copied from the B-29, and the Soviets used them as their heavy bombers until the 1960s. [10]

The Russians recognized that, without America's support, they would not have been able to defend themselves. According to the Russian historian Boris Vadimovich Sokolov, the Lend-Lease program played a crucial role in winning the war:

> On the whole the following conclusion can be
> drawn: that without these Western shipments
> under Lend-Lease the Soviet Union not only

would not have been able to win the Great Patriotic War, it would not have been able even to oppose the German invaders, since it could not itself produce sufficient quantities of arms and military equipment or adequate supplies of fuel and ammunition. The Soviet authorities were well aware of this dependency on Lend-Lease. Thus, Stalin told Harry Hopkins [FDR's emissary to Moscow in July 1941] that the U.S.S.R. could not match Germany's might as an occupier of Europe and its resources."
From Wikipedia.

In the south, the Allies attacked through Italy and in 1944 landed in Normandy, France. Hitler's NAZI-Socialist war in Europe ended on May 8, 1945.

World War II was not a continuation of the Great War. Hitler and the NAZI-Socialists did not care to even the score after losing the war with the allies in World War I. They objected to the Versailles Treaty and the punishing war reparations, but getting even was not on their agenda. NAZI-Socialist Germany attacked western Europe as a defensive strategic action to protect itself from being invaded by the Allies from France. World War II in Europe happened because Great Britain and France objected to Germany's land grabbing in central Europe.

Chapter 16. In Conclusion

The outcome of World War II, just as in all the wars, is written by the winners. Contrary to what the winners maintain, World War II in Europe was not against Fascism. It was for freedom in western Europe and against socialism. Tens of millions of people, soldiers and civilians, died, and an immense amount of wealth/assets were destroyed in the European war theater over a war between *two socialist countries*: NAZI-Socialist Germany and Communist-Socialist Soviet Union. When the war ended, the democratic United States and the Communist-Socialist Soviet Union had won.

The Soviet Union was by far the bigger winner. Without War World II, the Communist state would have collapsed by the 1950s. Instead, it benefitted from American technology—and German technology as well—and rebuilt its economy to be on a par with Western economies. It acquired new land, European land in Central Europe, and was marching on to conquer the whole world, changing it into a Communist Marxist-Leninism world. It acquired nuclear technology from the United States through spying and became a nuclear power. And even though it continued to steal Western technology, the Marxist-Socialist principles, when it comes to economics, will always fail and collapse as they did in 1989.

Great Britain and France, in spite of what you may think, lost. How come?

Does the British Empire exist today? After WWII just about all its colonies became independent: India, Malaysia, Nigeria, Jordan, Jamaica, Namibia, Rhodesia, Zimbabwe, Kenya, Somalia, Uganda, and many others.

France lost Morocco, Algiers, Tunisia, French Sudan, Niger, Senegal, Cambodia, Vietnam, Laos, and many more.

And who caused the British and French empires to collapse? Their former ally, the Soviet Union and the Communist-Socialist world movement. Communism-Socialism came to power through revolution. Why not emulate and perhaps even copy the socialist revolution to obtain independence from the colonial powers? And the World Socialist movement was there to help with know-how, propaganda, and weapons.

Churchill was the great defender of the British Empire. If he had known the outcome for the empire by fighting NAZI-Socialist Germany, would he have kept on fighting or sign a peace treaty? That we'll never know.

How many millions of people died in the newly independent countries, especially after Marxist-Socialism took over? According to *The Black Book of Communism*, Marxist-Socialism was responsible for 1.7 million deaths in Africa.

Socialism is the gift that keeps on killing.

After World War I, the German Empire, the Austrian Empire and the Russian Empire lost and disappeared. The

British Empire and France won. They divided the spoils between the two of them and left behind a ruined, indebted, and resentful Germany. As a democracy, Germany would not have started the second war, but the chaos of the failed Weimar Republic, the Treaty of Versailles, and the Depression provided a fertile ground for Hitler's National-Socialist movement.

Hitler didn't want revenge against the loss of the World War I. His goal was to create a great, new Germany and provide for the Germans a better life under the banner of socialism.

His overtures to Great Britain for an alliance, where Great Britain would keep hegemony of the seas while Germany would invade the countries to the east and eliminate Communism-Socialism in Russia, were ignored or misunderstood. But why should Great Britain give a free hand to Germany to become strong again and conquer the Soviet Union? Britain already *had* hegemony over the seas and didn't need Germany's approval. Besides, Communism-Socialism was not much of an issue in Great Britain.

France and Great Britain were the powers in Europe, and they didn't want to share their power with anyone else, especially with a new ambitious Germany, turning the clock back to 1914. And so, the two countries drew a line in the sand in Poland when confronted by a new revived NAZI-Socialist Germany under Hitler. Poland provided no strategic benefit to them, but Hitler they feared, and they were losing the war until the United States came to their rescue.

What would have happened if Hitler hadn't greedily invaded Czechoslovakia, provoking Chamberlain to stand up to expansionist Germany? Or if France and Great Britain hadn't acted and declared war? Hitler would have invaded Poland, maybe on the same date, September 1, 1939, or sooner. France and Great Britain would have raised hell, but two weeks later, the Soviet Union swallowed the other half of Poland. It was not only NAZI-Socialist Germany but also the Communist-Socialist Soviet Union that devoured Poland. Short of war, and against who, Germany and the USSR? what were France and Great Britain to do but protest to the League of Nations? Besides, it was a land war in Central Europe heading east, far away from France or Great Britain.

Maybe on the same date, June 1941, or earlier, Germany would invade the Soviet Union. A war between two socialist countries would have caused what problems for France and Great Britain? There could have been some, but there was the advantage that, if it were defeated, the Soviet Union and its communist propaganda would end in Western Europe. Or if Germany were defeated, there was a twice-defeated Germany, needing repair, an advantage for France and Great Britain. Without the intervention of the United States, Germany would have conquered the Soviet Union and ended communism, replacing it with NAZI-Socialism. The Third Reich would have become the largest country in the world and a superpower.

Hitler Was a Socialists

The war in the Pacific was inevitable. Japan had no choice but to attack the United States at Pearl Harbor after the sale of oil to Japan was cut off. Oil was and still is the energy that fuels economies and war machines. Imperial Japan was conquering the West Pacific, and although the Pacific is enormous, only one power can dominate it— either the United States or Japan. (Note: that situation is no different from what's going on in the China Sea today.)

The United States defeated Japan, even though the US was supplying two fronts with men and armaments. But by fighting only in the Pacific, the US might have shortened the war considerably. Perhaps the nuclear bomb would not have been needed, and Japan could have been blockaded until it screamed uncle.

Different outcomes. One we know all about, and the other we can only speculate about. That other world would have seen four superpowers: The Third Reich, the United States, colonial France and the British Empire. Without the Soviet Union around France and Great Britain would have retained their colonies. Would there be everlasting peace? Only in our dreams. With Marxism-Leninism dead, National-Socialism was the new political movement in the world. The Third Reich, after digesting Soviet Union territory, like any other socialist power, would have expanded internationally against China. Who knows? And the United Sates could have had become a National-Socialist country as well.

Either way, no matter, the outcome of Socialism is our lot in life, where freedom dies, just as in NAZI-Germany or the Soviet Union.

And if Hitler had won, the following was one of his dreams:

> . . . planned—in the empire of the future—to forbid smoking and introduce vegetarianism. [2]

Hitler seemed to be such a forward thinker. Smoking is bad for you and no meat eating. Sounds like the *Green New Deal* of Alexandria Ocasio-Cortez.

I mentioned earlier what he had in store for the Pope: Hanging. All religions would have been a NAZI-Socialist religion with *Mein Kampf*, the new Bible, resting on the altar. The Christian cross would have been replaced by the swastika.

The Third Reich would have been similar to Sparta. The new Spartans would be the pure-blood Aryan German race. They would be the supreme citizens with equal rights and privileges in the Reich. All other nations, especially the Slavs, would be the Helots, the working class.

Our history of World War II reflects the bias against *fake fascism* and for Communism-Socialism. I hope this book clarified how we were deceived, allowing Marxism-Leninism to continue unabated.

From *The Black Book of Communism*:

> The Nazis after all, never pretended to be virtuous. The Communists by contrast, trumpeting their humanism, hoodwinked millions around the globe for decades, and so got away with murder on the ultimate scale. The Nazis, moreover, killed off their victims without ideological ceremony; the Communists, by contrast, usually compelled their prey to confess their "guilt" in signed depositions thereby acknowledging the Party line's political "correctness." [9: pg xv]

I witnessed such confessions when I was young. I saw grown-up men asking for forgiveness on their knees for their trespasses against the Party, just to be thrown in prison to do hard labor anyway.

To get an idea of how the confessions were extracted, I suggest you watch the movie *Milada* [11] available to downstream. This is the story of Milada Horáková, a politician and member of the underground resistance against the NAZIs in Czechoslovakia, who survived incarceration by the NAZIs and was liberated by the American troops. Five years later after torture and forced *confession*, she was hanged by the Communist-Socialists in Czechoslovakia on trumped up charges of treason.

Diabolical lies have proclaimed the greatness of Socialism. From *The Black Book of Communism*:

> The Communists' participation in the war and in victory over Nazism institutionalize the whole notion of antifascism as an article of faith for the Left. The Communists, of course, portrayed themselves as the best representatives and defenders of this antifascism. For Communism, antifascism became a brilliantly effective label that could be used to silence one's opponents quickly. The defeated Nazism was labeled the "Supreme Evil" by the Allies, and Communism thus automatically wound up on the side of Good. [9: pg 22]

And so, the Marxism-Socialism survived claiming moral superiority over mankind. Unfortunately, they're not finished yet. The United States of America subjugation is their ultimate goal. If they succeed, there is no other America out there to offer support for our liberation, and serfdom, misery, poverty and death will follow.

I hope you understood that socialism, not fascism, is what caused all the deaths in the past century. And it is still around looking for new victims.

Next time someone tries to denigrate you by calling you a Nazi, point out to them that you are not a Socialist.

I hope this book brought to light the truth about the NAZI, Socialism and Communism, where freedom is forbidden, the population becomes serfs of the government, and anybody who disagrees or fights is incarcerated or killed.

The Socialist motto is:

"If you're not with us you're against us.
If you're against us, you will be:
Reeducated or Exterminated."

The End

If you enjoyed this book and would like to help other readers with your comments please write a review on Amazon, which I appreciate very much. Amazon books link.

For more information about my books and my art please visit my website: sandru.com or write me an e-mail at mit@sandru.com

References

1. "The Communism Manifesto" by Karl Marx and Friedrich Engels, with introduction and notes by Gareth Stedman Jones, published by Penguin Classics.
2. "Hitler" by Joachim C. Fest, translated from German by Richard and Clara Winston, published by A Harvest Book, Harcourt, Inc., A Helen and Kurt Book.
3. "The Rise and Fall of the Third Reich" by William L. Shirer, published by Simon & Schuster Paperbacks.
4. "The Speeches of Adolf Hitler" by Adolf Hitler, Amazon.com.
5. "Mein Kampf" by Adolf Hitler, published by Mariner Books.
6. "The Program of the Party of Hitler, the National Socialist German Worker's Party" by Gottfried Feder, published by Ostara Publications.
7. "Escape from Communism" by Dumitru Sandru, published by Chivileri Publishing.
8. "How Socialist was National Socialism" by Alan Brown, Amazon.com.
9. "The Black Book of Communism" by a variety of writers documenting the crimes against humanity committed by the Communist-Socialists, published by Harvard University Press.
10. "The second World Wars" by Victor Davis Hanson. Basic Books, Hachette Book Group.
11. "Milada" the movie, by Loaded Vision Entertainment.
12. "Gun Control in the Third Reich: Disarming the Jews and "Enemies of the State" by Stephen P. Halbrook, published by Independent Institute.

13. "Hitler's Empire: The Post-War Plan" by AHC, video documentaries.

14. This edited interview of Adolf Hitler by George Sylvester Viereck took place in 1923. It was republished in Liberty magazine in July 1932, https://www.theguardian.com/theguardian/2007/sep/17/greatinterviews1.

15. Vladimir Lenin Was Part Jewish, Say Declassified KGB Files http://content.time.com/time/world/article/0,8599,2077413,00.html

16. "Adolf Hitler" by John Toland, published by Doubleday & Company, Inc.

17. "The Big Lie: Exposing the Nazi Roots of the American Left" by Dinesh D'Souza, Regnery Publishing.

18. "Liberal Fascism: The Secret History of the American Left, From Mussolini to the Politics of Meaning" by Jonah Goldberg, Broadway Books.

19. "Hitler's Germany: Origins, Interpretations, Legacies" by Roderick Stackelberg, published by Routledge; 2nd Edition.

Other Books by Dumitru (Mit, DG) Sandru

Non-Fiction, Political

Escape from Communism, by Dumitru Sandru, a True Story and Commentary.

Life under communism is cruel and inhumane. Commit the smallest political infraction, and the secret police will arrest you. The only ray of hope is the West, but it is a crime to escape by crossing the border illegally, and anyone caught is beaten and imprisoned, sometimes even shot. This is my story of what happened and how I reached freedom.

Hitler Was a Socialist, by Dumitru Sandru, A Comparison of NAZI-Socialism, Communism, Marxism-Socialism, and the United States

We are socialists, we are enemies of today's capitalistic economic system for the exploitation of

the economically weak, with its unfair salaries, with its unseemly evaluation of a human being according to wealth and property instead of responsibility and performance, and we are determined to destroy this system under all conditions.

These are the words of Adolf Hitler. He and the National-Socialist German Worker's Party –the NAZI– was a Socialist Party. Then who told us that Hitler and the NAZI were Fascist? Joseph Stalin, the mass murderer of the USSR said so. And the rest of the world obeyed. It is time to uncover the truth.

Adolf Hitler was a monster, a Socialist monster, just like Mao Zedong, Joseph Stalin, Pol Pot, and many other socialists like them. The facts are out there in plain sight, but the Marxist Academia, Leftist Mainstream Media, and Hollywood will not consider talking about the truth, least it would tarnish the "good" reputation of the Socialism, which killed 200 million people worldwide.

Socialism we must fear, not fascism.

Paranormal, Mystery, Thriller

The Pregnant Pope (Book 1 TIO Series), by Mit Sandru.

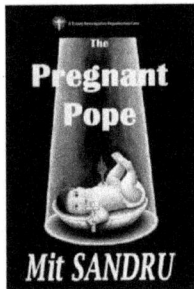

The 92-year-old Pope is pregnant. He hasn't undergone any medical procedures, but he carries a fetus in his abdomen. Is this a case of self-cloning, or a mutation? Is this an Immaculate

Conception, or Satan's work? Find out how Claire, Travis, and Prescott solve this mystery and the bizarre outcome.

The Devolution of Adam and Eve (Book 2 TIO Series) by Mit Sandru

A pandemic causes billions of people to lose their minds. The world's government health agencies cannot identify the pathogen and develop an antidote. It comes from another realm, and only Claire, Prescott, and Travis can solve this enigma. Will they prevent the end of humanity before it's too late?

Teen, Children Fantasy

Arboregal, the Lorn Tree, by D.G. Sandru. YouTube: **https://bit.ly/2OtDj5c**

Four youngsters, Melissa, Perry, Nathan and Michelle materialize in a desolate world where giant, mile-high trees, support all life. They find shelter in the Lorn Tree among the Lorns. Soon after they discover that an evil spirit, Hellferata, wants them dead. Fearful Lorns want to expel the youngsters from their tree, which would be a dead sentence since monsters roam the land at night.

Will their ingenuity, cunning, and courage help them escape, or will Hellferata mete out her wrath before they can escape?

<u>Science Fiction</u>

Sferogyls (Timurud Book 1) by Mit Sandru

The Maggotroll Empire invades the Sferogyls' planet. The Sferogyls are unarmed and have no defense against the imperial battleships. The gods resurrect Timurud and send him to help the peaceful Sferogyls fight the invaders. Will the Sferogyls win the war in space and defend their planet, or perish?

Gold Rush Mystery (Terraspantion Chronicles, Bk. 1) by Mit Sandru.

America is back on the Moon, and we intend to stay and establish a self-sustaining permanent base for tourism and mining. The work is challenging, the environment is deadly, but the astronauts Mia, Geo and Roby succeed in building the moon base, even if they landed in a mysterious crater.

Time Hole, (Terraspantion Chronicles, Bk. 2) by Mit Sandru.

Mining on the moon is a hazardous affair. Deedee and Arno, two lunar generalists, find perils beyond what they signed up for when they travel on the lunar surface at night . . . on the dark side of the Moon. Time will not be the same after they fall into the Time Hole.

Folding Reality, by Mit Sandru. Time Travel Adventure

Mike the insurance salesman experiences perilous time travel experiences just by folding a piece of paper. He is crucified on Golgotha, almost gassed at Auschwitz, marooned in a Russian capsule going to the Moon.

Vampires - Thriller & Romance
YouTube: https://bit.ly/2pahMDI
YouTube: https://bit.ly/2lPwAt4
Vampire (Vlad V, Bk 1) by Mit Sandru.

Meeting a vampire isn't something that happens every night, even on the New York City subway. But never in her wildest dreams did Cat Sanders ever expect to meet the vampire Vlad V Draculesti and survive the encounter. Instead, she became his confidant. Why was she so lucky?

R.I.P., The Death of a Vampire (Vlad V, Bk 2) by Mit Sandru.

Vlad V Draculesti is dying because of an incident that happened decades ago. Unfortunately for Vlad V, the US intelligence agencies investigate him to find out his true identity, and centuries old life. Will Cat Sanders and vampire friends be able to help him die in peace, or will Vlad be discovered for being a vampire and die in a US Federal research laboratory?

Vampire Slayers (Vlad V, Bk 3) by Mit Sandru.

Cat Sanders is a billionaire, but not all is well. Her nemesis, Veronica Seyler, allied with a vampire-slayer drug cult, demands extortion money or she will be killed.

Cat's vampire friend, Angelique, comes to her aid. But the cult is more cunning and dangerous than even her vampire friend could handle. Would Cat and Angelique be able to come out of this alive even if Cat pays the ransom?

Vampires of Transylvania (Vlad V, Bk 4) by Mit Sandru

Cat Sanders has a simple task: spread Vlad V's ashes in Transylvania at midnight, during full moon. But in Transylvania Vlad V has centuries old enemies who take her and her friend Tudor hostage, placing them in iron cages among zombies and proto-vampires. Will they be able to escape from the blood sucking proto-vampires and flesh-eating zombies, or become zombies themselves?

The Queen of Vampires: A New Queen Arises (Vlad V, Bk 5) by Mit Sandru

The Vampire Queen, Eleonore von Schwarzenberg, is bloodthirsty and vengeful on Cat Sanders and her friends. She

plans the most painful death for them. Cat and her friends find themselves entrapped and helpless to avoid her wrath.

Will Cat and her friends be able to escape and survive the Queen of Vampires' fury?

Coloring Book
Abstract Dreams: Coloring Book 1 (Sandru's Art) by Dumitru Sandru
YouTube: **https://bit.ly/2Ulc9RT**

Reward your soul with the smooth and pleasing lines of Abstract Dreams
https://www.sandru.com/Coloring.html

T-Shirts and other stuff:

https://www.zazzle.com/store/dgsandru/products

Dumitru Sandru

Visit my e-Gallery at:

https://www.sandru.com/SferogylsArt.html
https://www.sandru.com/LornTreeArt.html
http://dumitru-sandru.artistwebsites.com/
https://www.pinterest.com/mitsandru/

About Dumitru "Mit" Sandru

Mit Sandru was born in the greater area of Transylvania in the last millennium; make that last century since he's not a vampire. Yet. When he was six years old, a soldier shot him at point blank range with a Kalashnikov. He survived. He outsmarted his German teacher, and survived a tornado in the middle of a wheat field. Not concurrently. When he was 18 years old, he escaped from a country resembling a concentration camp, luckily without being killed. He outran mean border patrol dogs in a foreign country, in the darkness of night, while jumping over six-foot tall stonewalls. Superman he's not. He came to the USA in search of freedom, glory, wealth, and fame. He's still searching for three of those. Lightning grazed him, and he caught a shark by the tail. Once. A monkey attacked him in Japan, but his daughter saved him. He avoided many rattlesnake bites, and built a house. No relation between the snakes and the house. Life eventually tamed him and he became a responsible citizen, with a wife, two daughters, dog and cat. And lately two grandsons. The taming part is questionable. He acquired an engineering and management degree and attempted to acquire other degrees in music, marketing, and IT. A certified student he is. He obtained many professional licenses, which he hardly used, but looked good on his wall. At 59-¾ years old he quit the corporate life and a six-figure salary. Rumor has it that he was given the golden handshake. He was finally free to pursue his dreams of writing, painting and music. During his professional life he painted hundreds of canvases, and composed dozens of tunes, while since his golden handshake he wrote 14 books; although one is a coloring book. And that was in just the first half of his life.

Disclaimer: Everything written here is true, but the bullets were blanks.

I am Mit Sandru and I approve this unabashed bio.

Want to see and read more about the second half of his life?

Webpage: http://sandru.com
Twitter: http://bit.ly/1kVzh6Z
Facebook: http://on.fb.me/1OiYOCn
Goodreads: http://bit.ly/1TgVbNa
Amazon: Amzn.to/1UtpTFR
Pinterest: https://www.pinterest.com/mitsandru/
YouTube videos
Arboregal, The Lorn Tree:
https://bit.ly/2OtDj5c
Abstract Dreams: Coloring Book 1:
https://bit.ly/2Ulc9RT
Vlad V Vampire Series:
https://bit.ly/2pahMDI
Lucy the Vampire Dog:
https://bit.ly/2lPwAt4

CPSIA information can be obtained
at www.ICGtesting.com
Printed in the USA
BVHW081016241220
596449BV00012B/955

9 781942 612179